What Is Meaning?

SOOCHOW UNIVERSITY LECTURES IN PHILOSOPHY
Chienkuo Mi, General Editor

The Soochow University Lectures in Philosophy are given annually at Soochow University in Taiwan by leading international figures in contemporary analytic philosophy.

Also in the series:

Ernest Sosa, *Knowing Full Well*

What Is Meaning?

Scott Soames

PRINCETON UNIVERSITY PRESS

PRINCETON AND OXFORD

Published in association with Soochow University (Taiwan)

Published by Princeton University Press,
41 William Street, Princeton, New Jersey 08540

In the United Kingdom:
Princeton University Press,
6 Oxford Street,
Woodstock, Oxfordshire OX20 1TW

press.princeton.edu

Library of Congress Cataloging-in-Publication Data

Soames, Scott.
What is meaning? / Scott Soames.
p. cm. — (Soochow university lectures in philosophy)
Includes index.
ISBN 978-0-691-14640-9 (hardcover : alk. paper)
1. Meaning (Philosophy)   2. Proposition (Logic)   I. Title.
B105.M4S68 2010
121'.68—dc22
2010015510

British Library Cataloging-in-Publication Data is available

This book has been composed in Minion Pro

Printed on acid-free paper. ∞

Printed in the United States of America

1   3   5   7   9   10   8   6   4   2

To Martha
Without Which Not

Contents

Acknowledgments

THIS BOOK IS AN EXPANDED VERSION OF A SERIES of three lectures given June 8–12, 2008 as the second annual Soochow Lectures in Philosophy, at Soochow University, in Taipei, Taiwan, Republic of China. Chapters 2–6 are expanded versions of those lectures, to which chapters 1 and 7 have been added in the present book. I owe a debt of gratitude to the organizers and participants in the sessions for their help in making the event both enjoyable and successful. Particular thanks are due to the three chairpersons of the sessions: Chienkuo Mi, Associate Professor and Chair of the Philosophy Department at Soochow, Wen-Fang Wang, Professor at the Institute of Philosophy of Mind and Cognition, National Yang Ming University, and Cheng-Hung Lin, Visiting Professor at Soochow. Professors Mi and Wang, along with Cheng-Hung Tsai, Assistant Professor of Philosophy at Soochow, also shouldered the difficult task of translating the lectures into Chinese, and making them available to those attending the lectures. Without their generous efforts, the event could hardly have taken place. In addition, I owe a special debt to Professor Mi, who not only organized all aspects of the event, but was the driving force responsible for initiating and promoting the annual series of lectures. Finally, I must express my appreciation of the gracious and unstinting hospitality shown to me and my wife Martha by Professor Mi and his wife Yi-Chung Yeh.

What Is Meaning?

Chapter 1

Meanings

IN WHAT FOLLOWS, I will take it for granted that words, phrases, and sentences have meaning, that for each meaningful expression there are correct answers to the question "What does it mean?", and that two expressions mean the same thing when the answer to this question is the same for both. Theories of meaning envisioned by philosophers attempt to answer questions of this sort in a systematic way. The targets of such theories include formal languages of logic and mathematics, extensions of these languages incorporating philosophically important intensional and hyperintensional notions, fragments of natural language, and full-fledged natural languages. Although much progress has been made with these theories, much remains to be done.

This is as it should be. It's not the job of philosophers to inventory all of the semantically significant structure of English, or to note how it differs from that of Urdu. It is their job to articulate theoretical frameworks in which such investigations can profitably take place. Happily, these foundational efforts have not been wasted. Much of the progress so far achieved has occurred in frameworks descended from Frege, Russell, Tarski, Carnap, Kripke, Montague, Lewis, Stalnaker, Davidson, and Kaplan. However, the picture is not entirely rosy. There is, I shall argue, an unsolved problem at the heart of our conception of what meaning is, and what we want from a theory of meaning. My task will be to state the problem, indicate why it has been difficult to solve, and sketch the beginning of what I hope will prove to be a solution.

The problem involves the relationship between sentence meaning and the entities, called "propositions," with which such meanings have traditionally been identified. This notion is implicitly defined by the following assumptions.

A1.   Some things are asserted, believed, and known. These attitudes relate agents—those who assert, believe, or know something—to that which they assert, believe, or know.

A2.   The things asserted, believed, and known are bearers of (contingent or necessary) truth and falsity.

A3.   Propositions—the things satisfying A1 and A2—are expressed by sentences. The proposition expressed by S can standardly be designated by expressions such as ⌜the proposition that S⌝, ⌜the statement/claim/assertion/belief that S⌝, or simply ⌜that S⌝.

A4.   Since different sentences may be used to assert the same thing, or express the same belief, and since different beliefs or assertions may result from accepting, or assertively uttering, the same sentence, propositions are not identical with sentences that express them. Intuitively, they are what different sentences, or utterances, that say, or are used to say, the same thing have in common.

A1–A3 are little more than platitudes. By contrast, the abstraction implicit in A4 may seem worrying. What, after all, do different utterances that "say the same thing" have in common? Although the answer to this question is not obvious, the abstraction involved in attempting to answer it is not fundamentally different from other, presumably innocent, abstractions. What are the infinitely many meaningful sentences of a language, if not abstractions from the finitely many utterances of its speakers? Since there is no science of language without such abstraction, abstraction itself isn't a serious worry about propositions. As we shall see, however, there are deep and serious worries about propositions that go to the heart of the question of whether they can play the roles required of them in theories of language and mind, or whether, on the contrary, they should be dispensed with altogether.

In order to appreciate the force of this dilemma, one needs some sense of the roles that propositions do play in our theories. Within semantics, propositions are needed (i) as referents of certain names—'Logicism', 'Church's Thesis', 'Goldbach's Conjecture'; (ii) as referents of demonstratives in utterances of sentences like 'That's true'; (iii) as entities quantified over, as in sentences like 'At least six of the theses advanced by Professor Wyman are unsupported by evidence'; and (iv) as objects of the attitudes, as indicated by the sentence 'Mary defended several of the claims that Bill denied and Susan questioned'. Propositions are also needed to state the goals of semantic theory, and to relate semantics to the interpretation of speakers. Even if a language lacks propositional attitude constructions, we still need to know what speakers assert and believe, when they sincerely utter, or assent to, a sentence. Since propositions are that which is asserted and believed, and since semantics is charged with specifying the contribution of the meaning, or semantic content, of a sentence to what is asserted by utterances of it, propositions are presupposed by our best account of what we want semantic theories to do.

Recent advances in our understanding of the relationship between semantics and pragmatics have added to the weight placed on propositions. For many years, the governing assumption about the relationship between meaning and assertion was that *what a speaker asserts* when uttering a sentence is typically nothing more than *the semantic content of the sentence uttered*, plus, perhaps, a few trivially obvious consequences of this (e.g., the conjuncts of a conjunction). In the last two decades that picture has been complicated by the recognition (i) that the semantic contents of some sentences are incomplete, and require the contribution of pragmatic information available in the context of utterance in order to generate truth-evaluable candidates for assertion, and (ii) that even when the semantic content of a sentence is complete, that content can often be further enriched by contextually salient information. As a result of this semantic-pragmatic interaction, a single utterance of a sentence often succeeds in making multiple assertions, some of which go well beyond the semantic content of the sentence uttered; and in some cases, the semantic content of the sentence uttered is not even among the propositions asserted.[1]

---

[1] See my "Naming and Asserting," "The Gap Between Meaning and Assertion," "Drawing the Line Between Meaning and Implicature—and Relating Both to Assertion," and "Why Incomplete Definite Descriptions Do Not Defeat Russell's Theory of Descriptions,"

These observations pose a serious challenge to semantic theories that try to do without propositions by assigning each utterance, or sentence-in-context, a single set of truth conditions that determines a single truth value.[2] Since the truth value of an utterance can only be the truth value of the conjunction of all the assertions it makes—which, in turn, have been shown to contain a great deal of nonsemantic information provided by features of the context—any strictly semantic theory that assigns truth conditions directly to utterances faces the dilemma of either incorrectly assigning such utterances impoverished truth conditions (that leave out the pragmatic contributions of context), or incorrectly building nonsemantic information into meaning, often by mischaracterizing pragmatic contributions to assertion as semantic ambiguities (as in attempts to semanticize Donnellan's referential/attributive distinction). By contrast, the newfound recognition of the complex relationship between semantic and assertive content is made to order for a theory that

---

all reprinted, or initially printed, in my *Philosophical Essays*, vol. 1 (Oxford and Princeton: Princeton University Press, 2009). See also Kent Bach, "Conversational Impliciture," *Mind and Language* 9 (1994), 124–62, and "You Don't Say?," *Synthese* 127 (2001), 11–31; Anne Bezuidenhout, "Pragmatics, Semantic Underdetermination and the Referential/Attributive Distinction," *Mind* 106 (1997); Robyn Carston, *Thoughts and Utterances: The Pragmatics of Explicit Communication* (Oxford: Blackwell, 2002); Gennaro Chierchia, "Scalar Implicatures, Polarity Phenomena, and the Syntax/Pragmatics Interface," in A. Belletti, ed., *Structures and Beyond* (Oxford: Oxford University Press, 2004); Laurence R. Horn, "The Border Wars: A neo-Gricean Perspective," in K. Turner and K. von Heusinger, eds., *Where Semantics Meets Pragmatics* (Amsterdam: Elsevier, 2005); Stephen Neale, "Pragmatism and Binding," in Zoltan Szabo, ed., *Semantics versus Pragmatics* (Oxford: Oxford University Press, 2005), Francois Recanati, *Direct Reference* (Oxford: Blackwell, 1993); Dan Sperber and Deirdre Wilson, *Relevance* (Cambridge, MA: Harvard University Press, 1986); and Kenneth Taylor, "Sex, Breakfast, and Descriptus Interruptus," *Synthese* 128 (2001), 45–61.

[2] A good example of such a theory is Donald Davidson's, which, when extended to cover context-sensitive sentences, issues in clauses assigning unique truth conditions to every utterance of a sentence satisfying certain conditions. See pp. 49–50 of Donald Davidson, *Truth and Predication* (Cambridge: Harvard University Press, 2005).

takes the semantic content of a sentence to be a structured complex that provides a skeleton for the proposition, or propositions, asserted—which are arrived at by pragmatically fleshing out the bare bones provided by the semantics.[3] Without structured propositions, as contents of sentences, objects of attitudes, and bearers of truth value, it is hard to see how any suitably complex theory of the relationship between semantics and pragmatics could get off the ground.

Propositions are also ubiquitous in other areas of philosophy. For example, epistemological questions about what can be known, and about whether there are necessary truths that are knowable only aposteriori and contingent truths that are knowable apriori, presuppose that certain things that are known are also bearers of contingent, or necessary, truth. These are propositions. But if there is no denying the existence of propositions, there is also no denying the puzzles to which they give rise, and the problematic answers to those puzzles provided by traditional conceptions of them. Appeals to propositions in theories of language and mind incur the debt of explaining what it is for us to entertain, or otherwise bear cognitive attitudes to, them—and to identify that to which propositions owe their ability to represent the world, and so bear truth conditions. Traditional answers to the first of these questions are variations on the familiar story of

---

[3] See the first three articles in the first footnote. On Donnellan, see Keith Donnellan, "Reference and Definite Descriptions," *Philosophical Review* 75 (1966), 281–304; and "Speaker's Reference, Descriptions, and Anaphor," in Peter A. French, Theodore E. Uehling, and Howard K. Wettstein, eds., *Contemporary Perspectives in the Philosophy of Language* (Minneapolis: University of Minnesota Press, 1979); Saul Kripke, "Speaker's Reference and Semantic Reference," in French, Uehling, and Wettstein; Stephen Neale, *Descriptions* (Cambridge, MA: MIT Press, 1990); and my "Donnellan's Referential/Attributive Distinction," *Philosophical Studies* 73 (1994), 149–68, reprinted in *Philosophical Essays*, vol. 1.

propositions as denizens of a "third realm" (beyond mind and matter), which are "grasped" by a mysterious intellectual faculty of platonic extrasensory perception. Answers to the second question typically assume that propositions are both intrinsically representational, and that from which all other representational bearers of truth conditions—sentences, utterances, and mental states—inherit their representationality.

In what follows, I will explain why I have come to think that propositions in this traditional sense do not exist. If I am right, we face a dilemma. Either we must learn to conceptualize our philosophical, linguistic, and cognitive problems and theories without appealing to propositions, or we must conceive of them in a fundamentally different way. I will argue for the second horn of this dilemma by offering a new account of propositions that reverses traditional explanatory priorities. Propositions, as I understand them, *can* play the roles for which they are needed in semantics, pragmatics, and other areas of philosophy. However, they are *not* the source of that which is representational in mind and language. Sentences, utterances, and mental states are not representational *because* of the relations they bear to inherently representational propositions. Rather, propositions are representational *because* of the relations they bear to inherently representational mental states and cognitive acts of agents.

The view I will outline locates meaning in thought, perception, and the cognitive acts of agents. Although language is the locus of our ordinary and theoretical talk about meaning, meaning itself, or more properly, propositions—which are the meanings of sentences—are understood in terms of the explanatorily prior notion of agents predicating properties—of objects, other properties, and even of propositions—in all forms of cognition.

For this reason, I reject the pervasive "language of thought" fantasy, which wrongly takes linguistic meaning as the fundamental model—to be extended to theories of cognition—for understanding all intentionality. By contrast, I start with perception. One who sees an object x *as red* and tastes it *as sweet* thereby predicates redness and sweetness of it, just as one who feels an object y *as vibrating* and hears it *as humming* predicates those properties of it. As a result, the perceptual experience of the first represents x as *being red and sweet*, while that of the second represents y *as vibrating and humming*. In virtue of this, the first agent bears a propositional attitude to the proposition *that x is red and sweet*, while the second bears a similar attitude to the proposition *that y is vibrating and humming*. These perceptual attitudes, as well the perceptual beliefs to which they typically give rise, are usually not linguistically mediated.

The same is true of much—but not all—of our thought. As I have argued elsewhere, the introduction of language changes our cognitive calculus by expanding our cognitive reach.[4] In making objects and properties with which we may have had no prior acquaintance cognitively available to us, as well as providing the means of predicating the latter of the former, language vastly increases our stock of beliefs and other complex propositional attitudes. As a result, we come to believe, know, and doubt many propositions to which our only cognitive access is mediated by sentences of our language that express them. For this reason, language is not merely a means of encoding and communicating prior and independent cognition, but also a fertile source of

---

[4] Soames, "Semantics and Semantic Competence," *Philosophical Perspectives* 3 (1989), 575–96, reprinted in *Philosophical Essays*, vol. 1 (see, in particular, 194–200).

new cognition. Nevertheless, the explanatory model by which propositions—as meanings of sentences and objects of attitudes like assertion and belief—are to be understood is one that applies to cognitive acts of agents in their full generality, including the nonlinguistic acts of perceptual cognition, which form the basis for more complex, linguistically mediated, thought.

My route to this result begins with a discussion of the two main approaches to semantics in the tradition of Frege. According to one, theories of meaning are theories of *meanings*, or propositions expressed. According to the other, theories of meaning are theories of truth conditions, whether Davidsonian or modal. My first task will be to lay bare what appear to be insuperable obstacles to justifying either approach. After that, I will propose a solution to this crisis by sketching a workable theory of propositions.

Chapter 2

Frege and Russell

The Real Problem of "the Unity of the Proposition"

THE CLASSICAL TREATMENTS of propositions in philosophical semantics and psychology are those of Gottlob Frege and Bertrand Russell. According to both, propositions are meanings of sentences, bearers of truth, and objects of the attitudes. Despite this, they believed there to be a mystery at the heart of the proposition. For Frege and Russell, propositions are complex entities the constituents of which are meanings of the constituents of sentences that express them. Just as sentences aren't arbitrary collections of unrelated expressions, but rather have a structural unity that distinguishes them from other aggregates of expressions, so propositions aren't arbitrary collections of the meanings of expressions, but rather have a unity that distinguishes them from other aggregates of their parts. It is this unity that Frege and Russell find mysterious.

FREGE

Frege explains how the parts of a proposition "hold together" by distinguishing the senses of predicates from those of what he calls *proper names* (a category that includes both sentences and compound singular terms, as well as linguistically simple proper names). The senses of Fregean proper names are said to be complete, or saturated, while those of predicates are said to be incomplete, or unsaturated. The distinction is repeated for referents. Referents of proper names are called *objects*; referents of predicates are called *concepts*. These dichotomies are intended to be mutually exclusive. No concept is an object, and no unsaturated sense is saturated. Whether or not saturated senses can be referents of Fregean proper names is less clear. Although Frege sometimes seems to contrast senses in general with objects, he doesn't *need* to hold that saturated senses can't be referents of singular terms. Indeed, he takes thoughts, which are saturated senses, to be the indirect referents of sentences, which, for him, count as proper names. What does seem clear is that *unsaturated* senses, being incomplete, can't be referents of proper names, and so aren't objects, for him.

Frege's approach is systematic. Taking singular terms and sentences as basic, he obtains predicates by removing occurrences of singular terms from sentences. Since the resulting expression has gaps to be filled, its *sense* has similar gaps, into which the senses of singular terms (or of higher-order predicates) can fit, like pieces of a puzzle, to form a proposition. It is less easy to see what the incompleteness of *concepts* amounts to, especially after its paradoxical corollary that the concept *horse* is not a concept is pointed out. Here, Frege's discussion is shrouded in the fog of paradox. For him, this fog is nothing against the doctrines cloaked in it, but rather arises from the unspeakable depths being plumbed. We are invited to believe that what sounds false or paradoxical stems from limitations inherent in the use of language to explore its own foundations. Faced with this reality, it is only charitable, Frege thinks, to cut the truth-seeker some slack.

> By a kind of *necessity* of language, my expressions, taken literally, sometimes miss my thought: I mention an object [e.g., the concept *horse*], when what I intend is a concept. I fully realize that in such cases I was relying upon a reader who would be ready to meet me half-way—who does not begrudge a pinch of salt.[1]

However, the problem is not one of charity. The problem is the uncertain support for, and the dubious intelligibility of, Frege's doctrines. Before tying ourselves in knots trying to accommodate them, we need to look more closely at their content, and the arguments for them. What exactly is the problem of the unity of the proposition, and how—short of invoking the crude analogy of a jigsaw puzzle—are incomplete predicate-senses, and referents, supposed to solve it?

Frege states the difficulty as follows:

> It must indeed be recognized that here we are confronted by an awkwardness of language, which I admit cannot be avoided, if we say that the concept *horse* is not a concept, whereas, e.g., the city of Berlin is a city, and the volcano Vesuvius is a volcano. Language is here in a predicament that justifies the departure from custom. . . . In logical

---

[1] Gottlob Frege, "On Concept and Object," originally published 1892, translated by Peter Geach and reprinted in Peter Geach and Max Black, eds., *Translations from the Philosophical Writings of Gottlob Frege* (Oxford: Basil Blackwell, 1960), 54, my emphasis.

discussions one quite often needs to assert something about a concept, and to express this in the form usual for such assertions—viz., to make what is asserted of the concept into the content of the grammatical predicate. Consequently, one would expect that the reference of the grammatical subject would be the concept; *but the concept as such cannot play this part, in view of its predicative nature; it must first be . . . represented by an object.* We designate this object by prefixing the words 'the concept', e.g. 'The concept *man* is not empty.' Here the first three words are to be regarded as a proper name, *which can no more be used predicatively than 'Berlin' or 'Vesuvius.' When we say 'Jesus falls under the concept man,' then, setting aside the copula, the predicate is: 'someone falling under the concept man' and this means the same as 'a man.' But the phrase 'the concept man' is only part of this predicate.*[2]

He also says:

We may say in brief, taking 'subject' and 'predicate' in the linguistic sense: A concept is the reference of a predicate; An object is something that can never be the whole reference of a predicate, but can be the reference of a subject.[3]

In these passages, we are told that the *referent* of an expression that can be used predicatively can't be the referent of a singular term (Fregean proper name). We are also given the germ of two arguments, based on examples (1)–(3), for a crucial lemma needed to establish that view—namely, that the *sense* of an

---

[2] Ibid., 46–47, my emphasis.
[3] Ibid., 47–48.

expression that can be used predicatively can never be the *sense* of a singular term (or Fregean proper name).

1. Jesus is a man.
2. Jesus falls under the concept *man*.
3. *Jesus is the concept *man*.

Argument 1

P1.   (1) and (2) mean the same thing, as do their predicates, 'a man' (ignoring the copula in (1)) and 'falls under the concept *man*'.

P2.   The singular term 'the concept *man*' does not mean the same thing as the predicate 'falls under the concept *man*', of which it is merely a part.

C1.   So, 'the concept *man*' does not have the same *sense* as the predicate 'a man'.

C2.   More generally, no singular term has the same *sense* as any predicate.

Argument 2

P1.   If the term 'the concept *man*' in (3) meant the same as the predicate 'a man' in (1), then (3) would have a reading in which 'is' occurs as copula, and (3) means the same as (1).

P2.   (3) has no reading in which 'is' occurs as copula, and (3) means the same as (1).

C1/C2.   As before.

It is plausible to suppose that if these arguments were sound, then a stronger Fregean conclusion would also be forthcoming—namely that it is *impossible* for a predicate to have the same sense as a singular term. Even then, however, Frege's thesis

C3.   No singular term can refer to the referent of any predicate.

would remain to be established—since the claim that no expression in one class can have the same sense as any expression in another class doesn't, by itself, entail that no expression in the first can *refer* to the same thing as any expression in the second. Frege's argumentative route to C3 would, I suspect, invoke the idea that the function of a sense is exhausted by its role as a "mode of presentation" of a (potential) referent. Given this, one can rule out the possibility that C2 is true, but C3 is false. For, if that were so, then the sense of some singular term t would determine the same referent as the sense of some predicate P, even though the two senses were different modes of presentations of their common referent. But if the role of a sense were simply to present a (potential) referent—*without, in addition, encoding the semantic counterpart of the grammatical information about what in the sentence is predicated of what*—then there would be nothing to stop one from introducing a new singular term t′ (perhaps by stipulation) with the same mode of presentation as the one associated with P. Since this would violate C2, C2 plus the assumption that the function of a sense is exhausted by its role as a mode of presentation of a (potential) referent constitute a direct argumentative route to Frege's desired C3. In what follows, I will raise doubts about the first stage of the argument, in which he tries to establish C2.

The tacit assumption behind P1 of Argument 2 is that the grammatical structure of a complex expression makes no significant contribution to its sense. The phrases 'a man' and 'the concept *man*' are instances of different grammatical categories. The category to which the former belongs allows it to be combined with the copula to form a predicate; the category to which the latter belongs, we may suppose, does not. Thus, (1) and (3) have different grammatical structures—one being well formed with 'is' as copula, and one not. If the rules assigning senses to sentences are sensitive not only to the senses of their parts, but also to their grammatical structures, then there is no reason to think that (1) and (3) must have the same sense, if their parts do. Since Frege says nothing to exclude grammatical structure from being semantically significant in this way, P1 is unsupported, and Argument 2 is inconclusive.

Argument 1 is no better. Surely it is possible for someone to assert or believe that Jesus is a man, without having studied philosophical logic, and so without asserting or believing anything about objects falling under concepts. Since propositions are the objects of belief and assertion, (1) and (2) don't express the same proposition, and so don't have the same sense. The falsity of P1 also seems to follow from the Fregean doctrine that the sense of a compound expression E is a complex containing the senses of E's parts. On this view, the sense of (1) is a complex the constituents of which are the senses of the subject 'Jesus' and the predicate 'a man' (ignoring the copula). By parity of reasoning, the sense of (2) should be a complex consisting of the senses of the subject 'Jesus', the grammatical object 'the concept *man*', and the predicate 'falls under'. Since the senses of (1) and (2) contain different constituents, and have different structures, the claim that they don't differ in meaning is suspect. This is how Frege reasons in other cases.[4]

---

[4] See his discussion of the senses of A and $\ulcorner \sim \sim A \urcorner$ in "Negation," originally published in 1904, translated by Peter Geach, and reprinted in *Translations from the Philosophical Writings of Gottlob Frege*.

Consistency suggests it is how he should reason here as well.[5] That he doesn't is a measure of his commitment to his solution to the problem of propositional unity. But attachment to a conclusion is no argument for a premise that is supposed to support it.

Frege's conviction that no other solution to the problem of propositional unity is possible is expressed at the end of "On Concept and Object."

> Somebody may think that this is an artificially created difficulty; that there is no need at all to take account of such an unmanageable thing as what I call a concept; that one might . . . regard an object's falling under a concept as a relation, in which the same thing could occur now as object, now as concept. . . . This may be done; but anybody who thinks the difficulty is avoided in this way is very much mistaken; it is only shifted. *For not all the parts of a thought can be complete; at least one must be 'unsaturated', or predicative; otherwise they would not hold together.* For example, the sense of 'the number 2' does not hold together with that of the expression 'the concept *prime number*' without a link. We apply such a link in the sentence 'the number 2 falls under the concept *prime number*'; it is contained in the words 'falls under', which need to be completed in two ways—by a subject and an accusative; and *only because their sense is thus 'unsaturated' are they capable of serving as this*

---

[5] See pp. 14–18 of Jeff King, *The Nature and Structure of Content* (Oxford: Oxford University Press, 2007), for discussion of the tension generated by Frege's different remarks on this point, and the problems for his central doctrines posed by his claim that one and the same proposition—e.g., the proposition supposedly expressed by both (1) and (2)—can be exhaustively analyzed both as a unity of lower-order constituents and as a unity of different lower- and higher-order constituents.

link . . . I say that such words or phrases stand for a relation. We now get the same difficulty for the relation that we were trying to avoid for the concept. For the words 'the relation of an object to the concept it falls under' designates not a relation but an object; and *the three proper names 'the number 2', 'the concept prime number', 'the relation of an object to a concept it falls under', hold aloof from one another just as much as the first two do by themselves; however we put them together we get no sentence.* It is thus easy for us to see that the difficulty arising from the 'unsaturatedness' of one part of the thought can indeed be shifted, but not avoided.[6]

The boldness of the thesis here advanced contrasts with the weakness of the argument for it. The thesis is that every proposition must contain an unsaturated sense (which is neither expressed by, nor the referent of, any singular term). The argument is that since no sequence of singular terms makes a sentence, no structure of saturated senses of such terms makes a proposition—because nothing in such a structure is predicated of anything else. But this is a *non sequitur.*

Consider a non-Fregean analysis of the example (4), understood as containing the lexical items 'John' and 'human' as constituents, plus the copula 'is'.

4. $[_S [_N \text{John}] [_{VP} \text{is} [_{ADJ} \text{human}]]]$

The copula is here regarded merely as part of grammatical structure—something needed to form a sentence, which is not itself a sense-bearing unit. The proposition expressed by (4) is taken to

---

[6] "On Concept and Object," 54–55, my emphasis.

contain just two constituents: the sense of 'John'—which is, or determines, the man John—and the sense of 'human'—which is, or determines, the property *humanity*. Both may be referents of singular terms, and so qualify as complete in Frege's sense, provided that *something* about the proposition indicates that, in it, humanity is predicated of John. This something is, we may suppose, not itself a propositional constituent. Rather it is the structural relation in which the sense of 'human' stands to the sense of 'John' in the proposition. The constituents of the sentence provide the constituents of the proposition. The grammatical structure of the sentence provides the propositional structure that indicates what is predicated of what. Since Frege says nothing to rule this out, he fails to establish his doctrines C2 and C3, about incomplete senses and referents.

This is all to the good, since these doctrines cause nothing but problems. Consider, for example, Frege's account of quantification, illustrated by his discussion of (5a).

5a.   There is at least one square root of 4.

Frege says that in this sentence "we have an assertion . . . about a concept, *square root of 4*; viz. that it is not empty."[7] However, this analysis is rendered incoherent by his incompleteness doctrines. The analysis of the quantification in this example tells us that (5a) asserts something about a concept. The incompleteness doctrines tell us that since *the subject of this assertion* is a concept, it can't be the referent of a singular term. But this is self-refuting, since we have just made the concept the referent of the term, 'the subject of this assertion'. Note also Frege's identification of what is

[7] Ibid., 49.

asserted—namely, "that it is not empty." If 'it' here functions as a grammatical subject, then it is a Fregean proper name—in which case, his incompleteness doctrines compel him to deny that its referent is a concept, while his analysis of quantification requires him to affirm that it is one.

Here is the larger text in which Frege's self-refuting remark is embedded:

> *In the sentence [(5a)] we have an assertion . . . about a concept, square root of 4; viz. that it is not empty.* But if I express the same thought thus: 'The concept *square root of 4* is realized' then the first six words form the proper name of an object, and it is about this object that something is asserted. But notice carefully that what is asserted here is not the same thing as was asserted about the concept.[8]

In this passage, Frege says that the proposition expressed by (5a) can be taken in two ways: (i) as asserting (i.e., predicating) of a certain concept that it's not empty, or (ii) as asserting (predicating) of a certain object that it "is realized." Whatever the mysterious difference between *being non-empty* (predicated of the concept) and *being realized* (predicated of the object) is supposed to be, the doctrine is self-refuting. For Frege is committed to identifying the concept as the referent of the singular terms 'the subject of the first assertion' and 'the referent of the phrase *square root of 4*'.

The quoted passage continues in the same vein.

> Language has means of presenting now one, now another, part of the thought as the subject. It need not then surprise

---

[8] Ibid., 49, my emphasis.

us that the same sentence may be conceived as an assertion about a concept and also as an assertion about an object; only we must observe that what is asserted is different.
In the sentence [(5a)] it is impossible to replace the words
'square root of 4' by 'the concept *square root of 4*'; i.e. *the assertion that suits the concept does not suit the object.*[9]

Here Frege observes that whereas (5a) expresses a proposition
that can be used to make an assertion about a concept, (5b) cannot be so used.

5b.   *There is at least one the concept *square root of 4.*

For Frege, (5b) isn't well formed, because the sense of the quantifier requires completion by the sense of a predicate, rather than
by that of a "proper name." As usual, he ignores the possibility
that the ill-formedness of (5b) is a *grammatical* violation, and
that the reason (5b) doesn't express a proposition is that it lacks
a grammatical structure the propositional contribution of which
indicates that the higher-order concept given by the quantifier
is to be *predicated* of the referent of the grammatical predicate.
Since he ignores this explanation, his observations don't show
that his analysis, in terms of unsaturated senses, is correct.

He completes the passage as follows:

Although our sentence [(5a)] does not present *the concept*
as a subject, it asserts something about it [the concept]; *it
[(5a)] can be regarded as expressing the fact that a concept
falls under a higher one.*[10]

[9] Ibid., 49, my emphasis.
[10] Ibid., 49, my emphasis.

Here we get a third way of taking (5a)—as asserting (predicating) of the concept designated by the predicate that it has the relational property of *falling under* the higher-order concept designated by the quantifier. This, too, is incoherent, since it requires the subject of the assertion to be both a *concept*, and the *object* indicated by the subject of (5c).

5c.   The concept *square root of 4* falls under H. ('H' designates the higher-order concept.)

In sum, Frege's doctrines of unsaturatedness and incompleteness are neither established by his arguments, nor the solution to any coherent problem about the unity of the proposition. Although, as we shall see, there is an important philosophical problem in the background of his discussion, he hasn't identified it, let alone solved it.

RUSSELL

In *Principles of Mathematics*, Russell addresses similar concerns.[11] Like Frege, he takes the meaning of a predicate to play a key role in unifying the proposition. However, he rejects the idea that the meanings of predicates differ in kind from other propositional constituents. Instead he distinguishes *the way predicate meanings occur in propositions when they are used predicatively* from the way they occur when something is predicated of them. He says:

Terms which are concepts differ from those which are not, not in respect of self-subsistence [i.e., not by their very

[11] Bertrand Russell, *Principles of Mathematics* (New York: Norton), originally published 1903.

nature], but in virtue of the fact that, in certain true or false propositions, they occur in a manner which is different in an indefinable way from the manner in which subjects or terms of relations occur.[12]

The sentences in (6) illustrate his distinction.

6a.   Socrates is human.
  b.   Socrates exemplifies humanity.

According to Russell, the property humanity occurs in both propositions, but does so in different ways. In (6a), it is what is asserted, or predicated, of Socrates. Taking the proposition to be *about* Socrates, Russell says that Socrates occurs here *as a term,* whereas humanity does not. Since this is the only way Socrates can occur in a proposition, he counts as *a thing.* Because humanity can occur other than as a subject of predication, it is a *concept.* However, Russell maintains, everything can occur as a term in some proposition, as humanity does in proposition (6b).

In [6a], the notion expressed by 'human' occurs in a different way from that in which it occurs when it is called 'humanity', the difference being that in the latter case, but not in the former, the proposition is *about* this notion. This indicates that humanity is a concept, and not a thing.[13]

Next Russell adds something puzzling.

Thus, we shall say that 'Socrates is human' is a proposition having only one term; of the remaining components of the proposition, one is the verb, the other is a *predicate.*[14]

[12] Ibid., 46.
[13] Ibid., 45.
[14] Ibid., 45.

The term is Socrates, and the predicate is humanity. What is the verb? Russell returns to this a few pages later with the following difficult remarks:

> It may be asked whether everything that, in the logical sense we are concerned with, is a verb, expresses a relation or not. It seems plain that, if we were right in holding that [6a] is proposition having only one term, *the 'is' in this proposition cannot express a relation in the ordinary sense.* . . . . Nevertheless, a relation between Socrates and humanity is certainly *implied*, and it is very difficult to conceive the proposition as expressing no relation at all. We may perhaps say that *it is a relation*, although it is distinguished from other relations in that *it does not permit itself to be regarded as an assertion concerning either of its terms indifferently, but only as an assertion concerning the referent.*[15]

These remarks are confused. Russell should have said that proposition (6a) has two constituents, Socrates and humanity, the latter of which is *predicated* of the former. Although the proposition doesn't *contain* a third constituent relating the two, such a relation is *implied*, in the sense that the truth of the proposition requires Socrates to bear the exemplification relation to humanity.

Russell gets in another tangle in his discussion of verbs and verbal nouns.

> It is plain that the concept that occurs in the verbal noun is the very same as that which occurs as verb. . . . But . . . there is a further point. By transforming the verb as it occurs in a proposition [as concept, rather than as term], into a verbal

---

[15] Ibid., 49, my emphasis.

noun, the whole proposition can be turned into a single logical subject, *no longer asserted and no longer containing in itself truth or falsehood.* But here too, there seems to be no possibility of maintaining that the logical subject which results is a different entity from the proposition. "Caesar died" and "the death of Caesar" will illustrate this point.[16]

The problem Russell poses about assertion is, in the end, illuminating, but the example he uses to illustrate it is ill-chosen, since, on one natural interpretation, 'the death of Caesar' denotes an event in which Caesar dies, rather than a proposition. In order to keep confusion to a minimum, it will be useful to contrast the sentence 'Caesar died' with the clause 'that Caesar died' instead. The passage continues:

> If we ask: What is asserted in the proposition "Caesar died"? the answer must be "the death of Caesar is asserted." [Better: *that Caesar died* is asserted.] In that case, it would seem, it is the death of Caesar which is true or false [Better: *that Caesar died* is true or false]; *and yet neither truth or falsehood belongs to a mere logical subject. . . . There appears to be an ultimate notion of assertion, given by the verb, which is lost as soon as we substitute a verbal noun, and is lost when the proposition in question is made the subject of some proposition.*[17]

The mystery here is markedly diminished if the examples in question are related as in (7).

---

[16] Ibid., 48, my emphasis.
[17] Ibid., 48, my emphasis.

7a. Caesar died.

b. That Caesar died is widely believed.

Although this is not a case involving a verb and a verbal noun ('die' and 'death'), it is a case in which the proposition expressed by one sentence is what Russell calls "the logical subject" of the proposition expressed by another sentence. When applied to (7), Russell's comment that "neither truth or falsehood belongs to a mere logical subject" is clearly without merit, since the logical subject of (7b) is the true proposition that Caesar died.

It is, of course, correct that when one proposition is the logical subject of another, *asserting* the latter needn't involve *asserting* the former. But why is this worth noting? You would think it worth noting if you thought that *assertion* was what distinguishes a proposition from a mere collection of its constituents. For then, failing to *assert* the logical subject of (7b) would threaten Russell's account of its unity, which is just the unity of proposition (7a). Regrettably, Russell did write as if he believed something like this—as indicated by his remark that "in every proposition . . . we may make an analysis into something asserted and something about which the assertion is made."[18] Since many propositions are never asserted, this remark is, strictly speaking, false. However, one can easily see what is wanted—namely that in every proposition we may make an analysis into *something predicated*, and *something of which it is predicated*. Though related, predicating and asserting are different. When we *assert* proposition (7a), we both *predicate* dying of Caesar and *assert* of him that he died. However, when we assert (7b) we do the former without doing

[18] Ibid., 43.

the latter. It is *predication* that is central to Russell's account of the unity of the proposition, not *assertion*.

This brings us to his most famous remark on the subject.

> Consider, for example, the proposition "A differs from B." The constituents of this proposition, if we analyze it, appear to be only A, difference, B. *Yet these constituents, thus placed side by side, do not reconstitute the proposition. The differ-ence which occurs in the proposition actually relates A and B, whereas the difference after analysis is a notion which has no connection with A and B.* [my emphasis] It may be said that we ought, in the analysis, to mention the relations which difference has to A and B, relations which are expressed by *is* and *from* when we say A is different from B. These rela-tions consist in the fact that A is referent and B relatum with respect to difference. But A, referent, difference, relatum, B, is still merely a list of terms, not a proposition. *A proposi-tion, in fact, is essentially a unity, and when analysis has de-stroyed the unity, no enumeration of constituents will restore the proposition. The verb, when used as a verb, embodies the unity of the proposition, and is thus distinguishable from the verb considered as a term, though I do not know how to give a clear account of the precise nature of the distinction.*[19]

Again, the point Russell is groping for is clearer than his perplex-ing way of putting it—which he reiterates a few pages later, when he says, "Owing to the way in which the verb actually relates the terms of a proposition, every proposition has a unity which ren-ders it distinct from the sum of its constituents."[20] Part of the

---

[19] Ibid., 49–50, my emphasis.
[20] Ibid., 52.

point he is making in these passages is that there is more to the proposition that A differs from B than the fact that its constituents are A, B, and difference. In addition, there is both the manner in which these constituents occur in the proposition, and how their occurring in that manner *represents* the terms of the proposition as being a certain way. In the proposition, difference is *predicated* of A and B, with the result that they are *represented as being different*. In a mere list, nothing is *predicated* of anything, and so the list doesn't *represent* the items listed as being one way rather than another.

One might ask what we mean by 'predication'—what, in effect, the *analysis* of predication is. Although it is unclear that an informative answer can be given to this question, it is equally unclear that this is anything to worry about. Some logical and semantic notions—like negation—are primitive. Since this elementary point typically doesn't provoke hand-wringing, it is hard to see why the primitiveness of predication should. One might reasonably ask what, in a proposition, *shows* what is being predicated of what. At a general level, the answer is clear. Just as it is the structural relations holding among the syntactic constituents of a sentence that show how they are to be understood, so it must be the structural relations holding among the constituents of the proposition that show what it predicates of what. So far, then, we haven't found any serious problem of propositional unity.

THE REAL PROBLEM

However, we are not far off. There is a very serious problem awaiting us, for which nothing we have said provides an answer. What structural features of a proposition *do* show what is predicated of what, and *how*, exactly, do they manage to do that? Consider the proposition expressed by (8), the constituents of which are A, *difference*, and B.

8.   A is different from B.

In this proposition, the *difference* relation is predicated of A and B. What feature of the proposition shows that it is? Consider some candidates for being that proposition.

9a.   < difference, <A,B> >
  b.   { {difference}, {difference, { {A}, {A, B}}}}
  c.   < <A,B>, difference >
  d.   { { {A}, {A, B}}, {{ {A}, {A, B}}, difference }}
  e.   < difference, <B,A> >
  f.   { difference, {difference, { B, {B, A}}}}
  g.   < <B,A>, difference >
  h.   { { {B}, {B, A}}, {{ {B}, {B, A}}, difference }}

Any of these candidates could be used as a formal model of the proposition expressed by (8), as could any number of tree structures, a few of which are pictured in (10).

10a.

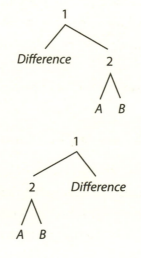

10b.

10c.

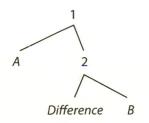

The problem is *not* that there is no determinate answer to the question

Q. Which of the structures of the sort illustrated by (9) and (10) is the proposition expressed by sentence (8)?

The problem is that it is hard to see how *any formal structure of this, or any other, sort* could be that proposition.[21] The proposition expressed by (8) is something that *represents A as being different from B*—by virtue of the fact that *difference* is predicated of them. But there is nothing in the sets or sequences in (8), the tree structures in (9), or in any abstract structure we might construct, or explicitly specify, which, *by its very nature*, indicates that anything is predicated of anything. Hence, there is nothing intrinsic to such structures that makes them representational, and so capable of being true or false.

We *could*, if we wished, adopt rules that would allow us to read off the needed information about predication from the structures, and so *interpret* them. To do this would be to *endow* the structures with representational meaning or content, thereby making them bearers of truth and falsity. However, it would *not* make them

---

[21] By a formal structure I mean a system of relations that organizes the constituents of the proposition in terms of relations that are not themselves semantically primitive or semantically defined, in a manner analogous to the way in which the syntactic structure of a sentence organizes its constituents in terms of grammatical relations that are not themselves semantically primitive or semantically defined.

propositions in the Frege-Russell sense. For Frege and Russell, propositions are *not* things that *have meanings*, or *get interpretations* from us. Rather, they *are* the meanings we assign to sentences, when we interpret them. The real problem posed by their confused discussions of the unity of the proposition is that their conception of propositions makes it impossible to answer the question *"What makes propositions representational, and hence capable of interpreting sentences by providing their meanings?"* Since no account of propositions can be accepted that doesn't answer this question, I conclude that if by 'propositions' one means what Frege and Russell did, then there are no such things.

Chapter 3

Why Truth Conditions Are Not Enough

IN THE PREVIOUS CHAPTER, I argued that Frege-Russell propositions don't exist, and so can't play the roles for which they were
designed, as bearers of truth, meanings of sentences, and objects
of propositional attitudes. With this in mind, we turn next to
theories of meaning that dispense with propositions. The central
notion in these theories is truth, of which sentences, or utterances of sentences, are the bearers. The guiding idea is that the
meaning of a sentence is given by its truth conditions. Although
there are different conceptions of what truth conditions are, and
how a semantic theory is expected to provide them, all leading
versions of this approach agree that the primary task of a theory
of meaning is to specify the truth conditions of sentences.

TRUTH WITHOUT MEANINGS

The original version of the approach was Rudolf Carnap's application of Alfred Tarski's theory of truth to the study of meaning, which was later extended to natural language by Donald

Davidson.[1] Both the central idea behind the approach and its most serious challenge are easily grasped. Since Tarski, it has been common to introduce interpreted formal languages by specifying a model and using a definition of *truth in a model* to assign truth conditions to every sentence of an uninterpreted formal system. This use of truth theories to *endow* sentences with meaning has encouraged the idea that they can also be used to *describe* the meanings of sentences in formal languages already spoken by working mathematicians. But surely, if truth theories can serve as theories of meaning for formal languages, there can be no principled objection to using them as theories of meaning for natural languages, too. There are, of course, daunting technical difficulties in implementing this idea, since an adequate theory of truth for the whole of a natural language would require numerous innovations not needed for the languages of logic and mathematics. However, there is a philosophical problem to be faced before going down this long technical road. The claim that one can give a theory of meaning for L by giving a theory of truth for L requires justification.

Consider again the use of a truth theory to *endow* sentences of a formal language with meaning. The announcement that we

[1] Alfred Tarski, "The Concept of Truth in Formalized Languages," and "On the Concept of Logical Consequence," in *Logic, Semantics, and Metamathematics*, 2nd ed., ed. John Corcoran (Indianapolis: Hackett, 1983); Rudolf Carnap, "Wahrheit und Bewahrung," *Acts du Congres International de Philosophie Scientifique*, Paris, 1936, translated as "Truth and Confirmation," in H. Feigl and W. S. Sellars, eds., *Readings in Philosophical Analysis* (New York: Appleton-Century-Crofts, 1949), 2–28; Carnap, *Introduction to Semantics* (Cambridge: Harvard University Press, 1942); Carnap, *Meaning and Necessity* (Chicago: University of Chicago Press, 1947, second, expanded edition, 1956); Donald Davidson, "Truth and Meaning," *Synthese* 17 (1967), 304–23, reprinted in *Inquiries into Truth and Interpretation* (Oxford: Clarendon Press, 2001); Davidson, "Radical Interpretation," *Dialectica* 27 (1973), 313–28, reprinted in *Inquiries into Truth and Interpretation*. (Citations will be to the reprinted versions.)

are using it to introduce an interpreted language contains a crucial piece of information not found in the theory itself—namely, that certain of its theorems *are to be viewed as providing paraphrases* of the sentences the truth conditions of which they state. Since this is no part of the truth theories themselves, it suggests that if they are to be taken to be descriptive theories of meaning, something beyond what they state must play a crucial role. Also, when we introduce interpreted formal languages, we typically don't have to choose which of the many theorems stating truth conditions of a single sentence provide *acceptable* paraphrases of it. Since potential paraphrases can often be proven to be extensionally equivalent, each serves the purposes of metamathematics perfectly well. This is not so when our purpose is to give a descriptive theory of meaning. So, if a Tarski-style truth theory is to fill the bill, it must be combined with something else that both provides the information that meaning-giving paraphrases are sought, and also specifies which of the many potential candidates are the genuine articles.

Davidson originally thought that a truth theory for L would count as a theory of meaning, if knowledge of what it states was sufficient for understanding L. The problem was in showing that his theories satisfied the condition. How can knowledge of a truth theory suffice for understanding, when its theorems give truth conditions of sentences only in the weak sense of pairing them with materially equivalent claims? If what one knows about S is expressed by the theorem ⌜'S' is true iff P⌝, one can readily conclude ⌜'S' doesn't mean that ~P⌝ and ⌜'S' doesn't mean that Q⌝, where Q is obviously incompatible with P. But how can one move from these modest negative results to interesting positive conclusions about what S does mean?

Davidson first thought that compositionality gave the answer. In compositional theories, theorems stating the truth conditions of sentences are derived from axioms interpreting their parts. So, he reasoned, "accidentally true" statements of truth conditions like ⌜'Snow is white' is true in English iff grass is green⌝ won't be generated without also generating falsehoods, like ⌜'Snow is grass' is true in English iff grass is grass⌝ and ⌜'Trees are green' is true in English iff trees are white⌝. Since truth theories must be *true* in order to qualify as theories of meaning, he thought that the problem of "accidentally true" statements of truth conditions wouldn't arise. Instead, he argued, truth theories that are both true and compositional will end up deriving only those statements ⌜'S' is true in L iff P⌝ in which P is a close enough paraphrase of S that "nothing essential to the idea of meaning . . . [would remain] to be captured."[2]

John Foster proved him wrong.[3] Let L_S be an extensional fragment of Spanish. Suppose that T1 is a true, compositional truth theory that delivers a *translational T-theorem*—⌜'S' is true in L_S iff P⌝ in which P means the same as S—for each S of L_S. We now construct a new theory T2 by replacing all axioms of T1 interpreting a word, phrase, or sentence-forming construction with new axioms stating different, extensionally equivalent, interpretations. Since T1 is both true and compositional, so is T2, despite the fact that *all* its T-theorems are nontranslational, like (1).

1.   'El libro es verde' is true in L_S iff the book is green and first-order arithmetic is incomplete.

---

[2] "Truth and Meaning," 26.
[3] J. A. Foster, "Meaning and Truth Theory," in Gareth Evans and John McDowell, eds., *Truth and Meaning* (Oxford: Clarendon Press, 1976), 1–32.

Knowledge of these theorems is clearly not sufficient to understand L_s. So, T2 can't be a theory of meaning, even though it satisfies Davidson's constraints. The problem remains, even if we assume constraints strong enough to rule out all but *translational truth theories*—defined as those that entail a translational T-theorem for each sentence of the language. Knowing what is stated by the translational theory T1 is no more helpful in learning L_s than knowing what is stated by the nontranslational T2—*unless one also knows, of that which is stated by T1, that it is expressed by a translational theory*. Thus, knowledge of what is stated by even the best truth theories is insufficient for understanding meaning.

Can we take a truth theory for L to yield a theory of meaning if knowledge of that which is stated by the conjunction of its axioms, plus knowledge, of this conjunctive claim, that it is stated by a *translational* truth theory, is sufficient for understanding L? No we can't, since even this knowledge *isn't* sufficient to understand L. One can know, of the relevant conjunctive claim, that it is stated by a truth theory that generates translational T-theorems, without knowing which of the infinitely many different T-theorems generated for each sentence is the translational one—and so, without understanding the sentence.[4] Nor is it sufficient to add something to a truth theory identifying the *translational* T-theorems. Although having all this information *would* enable one to understand L's sentences, the only role played by knowledge of the theorem labeled "translational" for a given S is that of identifying a claim in which S is paired with a content

---

[4] See Soames, "Truth, Meaning, and Understanding," *Philosophical Studies* 65 (1992), 17–35; reprinted in *Philosophical Essays*, vol. 1.

specified as that expressed by a translation of it. *Neither the truth of the translational T-theorem, nor the fact that it states the truth conditions of S, plays any role in this interpretation.* All it does is supply a mapping that could be provided just as well in other ways. One could get the same interpretive results by replacing the truth predicate in such a theory with *any arbitrary predicate F whatsoever.* Whether or not the resulting theory is true makes no difference. To interpret S, all one needs to know, of the claim expressed by the canonical F-theorem, is that it links S with *the content expressed by a translation of S.* Since this isn't enough for an F-theory to count as a theory of meaning, it isn't enough for a truth theory to do so either.[5]

The justificatory problem also can't be solved by turning it into a psychological theory, and attributing it to speakers.[6] On such a view, ordinary speakers unconsciously use truth theories to generate canonical T-theorems that pair natural language sentences with (antecedently understood) mental representations (in the "language of thought"). This won't do. In addition to the lack of empirical evidence supporting this psycholinguistic fantasy, speculation of this sort fails to address the basic justificatory problem. Even if, by purest luck, it were to turn out that English speakers used internalized truth theories as imagined, this *still* wouldn't justify taking them to be semantic theories of English. If a new speaker appeared, who assigned expressions the same internal representations we do, using a different method to do so, he or she would still be an English speaker. The job of a

---

[5] See Soames, "Truth and Meaning: In Perspective," in P. French and H. Wettstein, eds., *Midwest Studies in Philosophy* 32 (2008), 1–19; reprinted in *Philosophical Essays*, vol. 1.

[6] See Richard Larson and Gabriel Segal, *Knowledge of Meaning* (Cambridge: MIT Press, 1995).

theory of meaning is to tell us what sentences, and other expressions, mean. For this, it is irrelevant which of many conceivable psycholinguistic theories of sentence processing, or cognitive architecture, is correct.[7]

The final attempt to justify the claim that Davidsonian theories of truth can play the role of theories of meaning was inspired by some intriguing remarks of my colleague, James Higginbotham.[8] The idea is to augment a translational truth theory for L, so that it identifies a set CT of canonical theorems (including translational T-sentences), and specifies how knowledge of that which is stated by these theorems is related to understanding L. The suggestion is that such a theory counts as a theory of meaning for L iff it includes the true statements C1 and C2 about CT.

C1. For each theorem T_T of CT, knowledge of T_T is necessary for understanding L, as is knowledge that *knowledge of T_T is necessary for understanding L.*

C2. The knowledge specified in C1 is sufficient for understanding L.

However, this ingenious proposal doesn't work either. As I show elsewhere, C2 can't be true unless the *iterated* knowledge claim in C1 holds for translational T-theorems while failing for non-translational T-theorems (whether or not they are in the set CT designated by the theory). This condition is not met.[9]

The quickest way to see that it isn't is to note that for any translational theorem ⌜'S' is a true sentence of L iff P⌝ knowledge of

[7] "Truth and Meaning: In Perspective," 7–8; 232–33 in *Philosophical Perspectives*, vol. 1.
[8] James Higginbotham, "Truth and Understanding," *Philosophical Studies* 65 (1992), 3–16.
[9] "Truth and Meaning: In Perspective," 8–13; 233–38 in *Philosophical Essays*, vol. 1.

which is alleged to be necessary for understanding L, knowledge of the nontranslational ⌜'S' is a true sentence of L iff (P & 'S' is a sentence of L)⌝ will be equally necessary. Nor will the iteration clause of C1 make the needed distinction between these two T-sentences. Worse, the iteration clause is itself a source of further difficulty. The point may be illustrated using nonfactualism about mathematics. Nonfactualists hold that mathematical sentences of English, like those formulating Fermat's Last Theorem, don't have truth conditions. Thus, they reject the T-theorem ⌜'S' is true in English iff S⌝ for any such sentence S. I believe three things about nonfactualists: (i) they are wrong, mathematical sentences do have truth conditions; (ii) they sincerely don't believe, and so don't know, that these sentences have truth conditions; and (iii) they nevertheless are competent speakers, and so do understand the mathematical sentences about which they hold mistaken theoretical views. Given (i) and (iii), it doesn't matter whether I am right about (ii). If I am, then knowledge of truth-conditional theorems is not always a necessary condition for understanding sentences; if I'm not right—and nonfactualists really *do* know that mathematical sentences have truth conditions, despite sincerely denying this—then the mere fact that I take them at their word, while continuing to recognize them as competent speakers of English, means that *I don't believe* that knowledge of truth-conditional theorems is necessary for understanding. *Since this surely doesn't mean that I don't understand the mathematical sentences (to which I assign all the right truth conditions)*, the iterated knowledge condition in C1 fails. It is *not* a necessary condition for understanding S that one believe, let alone know, that knowledge of the truth conditions of S is necessary for understanding S. Thus, like every other attempt to justify the claim that Davidsonian truth theories may function as theories of meaning, Higginbotham's ingenious strategy fails.

This negative result leaves us in an awkward position. As I pointed out in chapter 1, there are two main approaches in philosophical semantics. According to one, theories of meaning are theories of *meanings*, which, in the case of sentences, are propositions expressed. According to the other, theories of meaning are theories of the truth conditions of sentences. The problem with the first approach—as practiced by Frege and Russell—is that we have no satisfactory conception of what propositions are. It is not, as I emphasized, that there are *too many* abstract structures that can play the role of propositions in our theories. The problem is that there are *too few*. We have no understanding of how *any* of the structures with which propositions might be identified could be inherently representational, and hence bearers of truth conditions—which they must be, if they are to be interpretations of sentences, rather than simply further things that themselves require interpretation. Recognizing this led us to the truth-conditional conception of meaning, only to find that Davidson's version of this conception suffers from a crippling defect of its own. Since his truth theories neither state what sentences mean— by issuing theorems ⌜'S' means that P⌝—nor pair sentences with entities that are their meanings, there is an immediate problem in justifying their status as theories of meaning. Davidson's attempt to solve this problem—by relating the information provided by a correct truth theory for a language to that which is necessary, or sufficient, to understand the language—was, I think, the only reasonable strategy for attacking it. The fact that pursuing this strategy for four decades has resulted in nothing but failure is good reason to believe that the justificatory problem can't be solved. Davidsonian theories of truth conditions *can't* be theories of meaning, because the semantic information they provide is too impoverished.

WHY MEANINGS ARE NOT CONSTRUCTED FROM TRUTH-SUPPORTING CIRCUMSTANCES

There are, of course, other truth-conditional theories, which, unlike Davidson's, assign truth conditions to sentences relative to an index. For languages without indexicals or other semantically context-sensitive expressions, the index is a circumstance of evaluation. For languages with indexicals, indices include both a *context of utterance* and a *circumstance of evaluation*—both of which, in turn, may contain various subconstituents depending on the richness of the language (and the particular theoretical approach taken to certain issues). Since the philosophical issues that concern us here are not affected by these technicalities, we can focus on simple, indexical-free, modal languages for which circumstances of evaluation are world-states. These are the elements relative to which quantifiers have domains, expressions have extensions, and sentences have truth values. A model for such a language consists of (i) a set W of world-states, (ii) a relation on W, relating w_1 to w_2 iff w_2 is possible from, or relative to, w_1, (iii) a world-state designated as "the actual world-state," (iv) a set I of possible individuals, and an assignment, to each w of W, of a subset of I as the domain of quantification for w, and (v) a valuation function assigning an *intension* to each nonlogical symbol s, where the intension of s is itself a function that maps each member w of W to the extension of s at w. A theory of truth is gotten by adding such a model to a compositional theory of truth conditions, relative to a model. This results, for each sentence S and structural-descriptive-name S_Q of S, in a modal T-statement (2) that specifies what the world *must* be like if S is to be true.

2. For all world-states w, S_Q is true at w iff at w, P.

It also results in an assignment of semantic contents (intensions/meanings) to each complex expression e. The intension/meaning of e is a function from world-states to extensions of e at those states. For example, the intension/meaning of S is a function from world-states to the properties truth and falsity, which is identified with the proposition that S expresses.

It is standard to take the world-states required by such theories to be metaphysically possible. However, when one appreciates what world-states are, it is easy to see that this isn't the only, or even the most plausible, choice. A world-state is *a way for the world to be*—a consistent, maximally informative property ascribed to the universe. It is metaphysically possible iff it is *a way the world could have been*—a consistent, maximally informative property that the universe could have had. It is epistemically possible iff it is *a way we can conceive of the world being, which we can't know apriori it isn't*—i.e., a consistent, maximally informative property we can conceive the universe as having, which we can't know apriori that it doesn't have. It is actual iff it is *the way the world is*—iff it is the consistent, maximally informative property that the world does have.[10] On this account, the metaphysically possible world-states constitute a proper subclass of the epistemically possible world-states.[11]

---

[10] For discussion, see Soames, "Actually," *The Aristotelian Society*, supplementary volume 81 (2007), 251–77; reprinted in Soames, *Philosophical Essays*, vol. 2 (Oxford and Princeton: Princeton University Press), 2009.

[11] See "Actually" for potential complications.

Which of these classes figures in a theory of truth affects the informativeness of its modal T-theorems. When world-states are restricted to the metaphysically possible, theorem (2) will be true iff the claim made by P is necessarily equivalent to the one made by S. Thus, one who knows that which (2) states can, in principle, narrow down the choice of S's potential meanings to a class of necessarily equivalent contents. Although this still isn't enough to enable one who knows the truth theory to identify what S does mean, it brings one closer to doing so than knowledge of a Davidsonian truth theory does.

In fact, we can do better. As I have argued elsewhere, there are good reasons to take truth-conditional theories of modal languages to range over epistemically possible, as well as meta-physically possible, world-states.[12] When this is done, (2) will be true iff the claim made by P is true at every epistemically possible world-state at which the claim made by S is true. Since many necessary truths are false at some epistemically possible world-states, the relationship between the content of P and the content of S, required by the truth of (2), is tighter than if metaphysically impossible world-states weren't allowed. Thus, adding such states increases the informativeness of truth-conditional theories, and narrows the range of ignorance about meaning that is consistent with knowledge of the truth conditions they state.

However, it doesn't eliminate all such ignorance. Since sentences with different meanings may express different, apriori equivalent, propositions, knowledge of these truth-conditional

---

[12] Chapters 3 and 6 of Soames, *Philosophy of Language* (Oxford and Princeton: Princeton University Press, 2010).

theories is not sufficient for understanding meaning.[13] This is illustrated by the modal T-sentence (3), which creates the same problem for taking theories of truth at a world-state to be theories of meaning that its predecessor did for Davidsonian theories.

3. For all epistemically possible world-states w, 'El libro es verde' is a sentence of L_S that is true at w iff at w, the book is green and first-order arithmetic is incomplete.

Could one argue that, unlike Davidsonian theories—which don't posit *meanings* and so have to rely on claims about *understanding* to justify their status as theories of meaning—theories of truth at a world-state, which do identify meanings, can be justified in some other way? In the abstract, this might seem to be a possible strategy. If there really are entities that are the meanings of sentences, then it is conceivable that a theory might correctly identify them, even if knowledge of the theoretical descriptions of those meanings provided by the theory wasn't sufficient to allow one to understand the sentences. However, this observation is of no help to a theory of truth at an epistemically possible world-state that identifies the meaning of a sentence with a function from such world-states to truth values. Since this theory wrongly assigns *all (non-indexical) apriori truths* the same meaning, it can't be correct.

The situation is even worse than it seems. The extra informativeness achieved by relativizing theories of truth to epistemically, rather than metaphysically, possible world-states may encourage

---

[13] When indexicals are involved, the relationship between apriori equivalence and truth in the same epistemically possible worlds breaks down. See "Actually" and chapter 6 of *Philosophy of Language* for discussion of the relevant complications. Since these don't affect the philosophical issues at stake here, they can be ignored.

the idea that making circumstances of evaluation even more fine-grained may enable us to construct a theory of truth that really does qualify as a theory of meaning. This was the hope of Jon Barwise and John Perry, when they developed situation semantics, twenty-seven years ago.[14] It was the failure of this hope that showed, once and for all, that no theory of the truth conditions of sentences relative to circumstances of evaluation can be a theory of meaning. The basic result is that no theory satisfying certain well-motivated assumptions can identify the semantic contents of sentences (the propositions they express) with functions from circumstances to truth values, no matter how fine-grained the circumstances are taken to be—provided that the theory preserves certain standard clauses of truth characterizations, such as those which state that a conjunction is true in a circumstance E iff both conjuncts are true in E, and that an existential generalization $\ulcorner \exists x \ Fx \urcorner$ is true in E iff Fx is satisfied by some object o in E.[15] Since these clauses are essential to truth theories, there is no hope of taking such theories to be theories of meaning, or of extracting the meanings of sentences (or the propositions they express) from them.

This result pushes us back toward Frege and Russell. The reason truth-conditional intensions can't serve as meanings is that they don't encode the syntactic structure of sentences, or other complex expressions. Any semantic theory that posits meanings as entities has no choice but to take the meanings of sentences to

---

[14] Jon Barwise and John Perry, *Situations and Attitudes* (Cambridge, MA: MIT Press, 1983).

[15] Soames, "Direct Reference, Propositional Attitudes, and Semantic Content," *Philosophical Topics* 15 (1987), 47–87; and "Why Propositions Can't Be Sets of Truth-Supporting Circumstances," *Journal of Philosophical Logic* 37 (2008), 267–76, both reprinted in *Philosophical Essays*, vol. 2.

be structured propositions that either encode, or are composed out of, the meanings of their semantically significant parts. For Russell, these were objects and properties; for Frege, they were saturated and unsaturated senses.[16] But once we adopt this structured view of propositions, we are faced with the problem that drove us away from Frege and Russell in the first place—namely, explaining how the entities we identify as propositions can possibly represent anything.

It can be argued that, after we moved beyond Davidson, it was an illusion to suppose that this problem ever left us. Theories of truth at a circumstance of evaluation identify sentence meanings, and propositions expressed, with functions from circumstances to truth values. When bivalence is assumed, the proposition expressed by a sentence can be identified with the set of circumstances in which it is true—though the set of circumstances in which it is false would technically be just as effective. There is nothing about any of these things—functions or sets—that makes them inherently representational. Individual world-states

---

[16] The considerations advanced here don't rule out taking meanings of complex expressions to be tree structures, the nodes of which are associated with the truth-conditional intensions of the corresponding constituents. However, if this route is taken, one must allow for the possibility that sometimes syntactically simple constituents (including individual words) can introduce complex intensional structures—as when a simple word like 'fortnight' is stipulated to be synonymous with a complex phrase like 'a period of 14 days'. In addition, one must find some way of avoiding set-theoretic paradox in giving the meanings of attitude ascriptions about attitude ascriptions—e.g., beliefs about beliefs. The intension of 'believe' is a function from circumstances to sets of pairs consisting of an agent and a structured proposition believed, which, on this account, is a structure of intensions. Given the familiar set-theoretic account of functions and pairs, we get the result that, when the intension of 'believe' is a constituent of the structured proposition/ intension believed, the intension of 'believe' will be a member of a member . . . of itself— which is paradoxical. Finally, the best account of what circumstances of evaluation are is one according to which they are built up from, and explained in terms of, objects and properties (see "Actually" and chapter 6 of *Philosophy of Language*), in which case properties shouldn't be explained in terms of them, as they, in effect, are, under this proposal.

are properties, as are other circumstances of evaluation, and so are not the kinds of things to be either true or false. Nor are sets of them, no matter how big. Thus if propositions are what they are standardly taken to be—inherent bearers of truth conditions from which both the sentences and the mental states of agents that express them derive their truth conditions—then propositions can't literally be sets of truth-supporting circumstances. The same is true of functions that map such circumstances onto truth and falsity. One might have thought that such sets, or functions, could at least serve as good formal models of propositions. However, we have seen that they are too coarse-grained even for that. Consequently, we still have no workable conception of the meanings of sentences, or the propositions they express.

Chapter 4

Propositions and Attitudes:
Davidson's Challenge
and Russell's Neglected Insight

THE PROBLEM WE FACE can be made clearer by examining propositional attitude ascriptions. On the face of it, attitudes like belief and assertion are relations between agents and the things—called 'propositions'—that they believe or assert. Thus, the natural clause in a truth-conditional semantics for attitude ascriptions is something along the lines of AA.

AA.   An attitude ascription ⌜x v's that S⌝ is true relative to an assignment A of i to 'x' and a circumstance of evaluation E iff in E, i bears the relation R (expressed by v) to the proposition expressed by S relative to A.

We know, from the results reviewed in chapter 3, that the propositions required by AA can't be sets of truth-supporting circumstances, or functions from circumstances to truth values (since, for any choice of such circumstances, substitution of truth-conditionally equivalent sentences in attitude ascriptions sometimes changes truth value). Instead, structured propositions are required. With this in mind, we can, in accordance with much contemporary practice, construct a two-stage semantics for a simple formal language. Stage 1 assigns structured propositions to sentences, while stage 2 is a theory of truth for propositions at a possible world-state. (The formal structures with which propositions are here identified are merely heuristically convenient choices; better candidates will be discussed in later chapters.)

Stage 1

a. The proposition expressed by an atomic formula $\ulcorner Pt_1 \ldots t_n \urcorner$ relative to an assignment A is $<P^*, <o_1 \ldots o_n>>$, where P^* is the property expressed by P, and $o_i \ldots$ is the referent of t_i relative to A.

b. The proposition expressed by a formula $\ulcorner [\lambda vS]t \urcorner$ relative to A is $<g, <o>>$, where o is the referent of t relative to A, and g is the function from individuals o' to propositions expressed by S relative to an assignment A' that assigns o' as the referent of v, and otherwise agrees with A.

c. The propositions expressed by $\ulcorner \sim S \urcorner$ and $\ulcorner S\&R \urcorner$ relative to A are $<NEG, Prop S>$ and $<CONJ, <Prop S, Prop R>>$, where Prop S and Prop R are the propositions expressed by S and R relative to A, and NEG and CONJ are the properties *being untrue* and *being jointly true*, respectively. Similarly for other truth-functional compounds.

d. The proposition expressed by $\ulcorner \exists v S \urcorner$ relative to A is $<SOME, g>$, where SOME is the property of being a propositional function that assigns a true proposition as value to some object as argument, and g is as in (b).

e. The proposition expressed by $\ulcorner$t believes that S$\urcorner$ relative to A is <BELIEVE, <o, Prop S>>, where BELIEVE is the belief relation, o is the referent of t relative to A, and Prop S is the proposition expressed by S relative to A.

Stage 2

a. A proposition <P*, <o_1 ... o_n>> is true at a world-state w iff P* is true of <o_1 ... o_n> at w.

b. A proposition <g, <o>> is true at w iff g(o) is true at w.

c. A proposition <NEG, Prop S> is true at w iff Prop S is false (not true) at w; <CONJ, <Prop S, Prop R>> is true at w iff both Prop S and Prop R are true at w. Similarly for other truth-functional compounds.

d. A proposition <SOME, g> is true at w iff for some object o at w, g(o) is true at w.

e. A proposition <BELIEVE, <o, Prop S>> is true at w iff at w, o believes Prop S.

The effect of adding propositions to the truth theory in this way can be seen by comparing (1a–c), which are consequences of these rules, with (2), which isn't.

1a. If 'John believes that someone loves Mary' is true at w, then there is a proposition that John believes at w which is true at any world-state w* iff someone loves Mary at w*.

 b. If 'John believes that someone loves Mary' is false at w, then there is a proposition that John does *not* believe at w which is true at any world-state w* iff someone loves Mary at w*.

    c.   There is a proposition p which is true at a world-state w* iff someone loves Mary at w*, and ('John believes that someone loves Mary' is true at a world-state w iff at w, John believes p).

  2.   'John believes that someone loves Mary' is true at w, iff (there is a proposition p that John believes at w which is true at any world-state w* iff someone loves Mary at w*).

Although (1a), (1b), and (1c) are true, the right-to-left version of (2) fails. Since a person can believe a proposition p that is true at all and only world-states at which q is true, without thereby believing q, (2) is false. The avoidance of this falsehood is our reward for moving from a conception of propositions as unstructured sets of truth-supporting circumstances to a conception of propositions as structured complexes of objects and properties.

The reward is paid for by weakened predictions about which attitude ascriptions follow from which others. One example of a prediction we would like to make is given by (3).

  3.   For any sentences S and R, if ⌜John believes that S & R⌝ is true at w, then so are both ⌜John believes that S⌝ and ⌜John believes that R⌝.

We could, of course, secure this prediction by adding a postulate—as part of our account of what the belief relation is—that one who believes a conjunction believes both conjuncts. Presumably, other facts could be handled in a similar way. Still, if our task is to interpret the ascription 'John believes that someone loves Mary', we don't have all the information we need. The only thing (1a), (1b), and (1c) do is locate what John must believe as being *somewhere* in a certain set of necessarily and apriori equivalent propositions. This falls short not only of giving the *meaning* of the belief ascription, but also of providing the *informative* truth conditions we are looking for.

At this point, we are apt to be reminded that (4) is also a consequence of the two-stage theory.

4. 'John believes that someone loves Mary' is true at w iff at w, John believes <SOME, g>, which is an ordered pair, the first coordinate of which is the property of being a propositional function that assigns a true proposition as value to some object as argument, and the second coordinate of which is the function g that assigns to any object o the ordered pair the first coordinate of which is the relation of loving and the second coordinate of which is the pair the first and second coordinates of which are o and Mary, respectively.

Here we face an embarrassment. Although we might want (4) to play a central role in interpreting the attitude ascription on its left, it can't do that because the interpretive clause on its right is so theory-laden as to itself require interpretation—and to be uninterpretable without it.[1]

---

[1] The problem posed by (4) for semantic analyses of attitude ascriptions that invoke structured propositions is a version of a more general problem that also arises for certain analyses of attitude ascriptions within the Davidsonian program—the most promising of which is that given in Richard Larson and Peter Ludlow, "Interpreted Logical Forms," *Synthese* 95 (1993), 305–56, reprinted in Peter Ludlow, ed., *Readings in the Philosophy of Language* (Cambridge, MA: MIT Press, 1997). The application of this problem to their proposal is discussed in chapter 7 of my *Beyond Rigidity* (New York: Oxford University Press, 2002), and also in my "Truth and Meaning: The Role of Truth in the Semantics of Propositional Attitude Ascriptions," in Kepa Korta and Jesus M. Larrazabal, eds., *Proceedings of the 7th International Colloquium on Cognitive Science* (Dordrecht: Kluwer, 2003), 21–44. This article also contains a generalization of the problem to semantic theories that take the objects of the attitudes to be structured propositions. Although a few positive suggestions are made there for solving this problem for structured propositions, the steps taken are incomplete and do not approach the genuine solution I will offer below in chapters 6 and 7.

This is, I believe, an instance of the problem Donald Davidson had in mind forty-three years ago when he made the following remark in "Truth and Meaning":

> Paradoxically, the one thing meanings do not seem to do is oil the wheels of a theory of meaning—at least as long as we require of such a theory that it non-trivially give the meaning of every sentence in the language. My objection to meanings in the theory of meaning is not that they are abstract or that their identity conditions are obscure, but that they have no demonstrated use.[2]

In speaking of meanings, Davidson was, in the first instance, referring to propositions. Although he was thinking primarily of Fregean propositions, his point applies to other accounts of propositions as well. His complaint was that positing meanings of expressions as constituents of a structured proposition P, identified as the meaning of a sentence S, is of no help in constructing a semantic theory, if one can't come to understand *what S means*, in the sense of identifying precisely how S represents things to be, by reading this off from the specification of P. Since this information *can't* be read off Fregean, Russellian, or any other standard theories of structured propositions, Davidson's criticism is a powerful objection to such theories.[3]

We are, of course, free to adopt rules that, in effect, interpret the things identified as structured propositions by assigning them truth conditions, as our two-stage semantic theory does. However, this is of limited help in extracting, from the

---

[2] "Truth and Meaning," 21–22.
[3] I discuss Davidson's criticism in "Truth and Meaning: In Perspective."

T-theorem (4), the information we need to interpret the attitude ascription 'John believes that someone loves Mary'. Applying the theory of truth for propositions to the ordered pair identified in (4) as the proposition believed is what gave us the theorems (1a), (1b), and (1c), which—as we saw—leave us ignorant of what we need to know. Although we need propositions as meanings of sentences and objects of the attitudes, and although these propositions must either encode, or be composed of, the meanings of the constituents of the sentences that express them, simply selecting abstract structures meeting these conditions, and providing a truth theory for them of the same general sort as has often been provided for sentences, leaves us far short of what we need in a theory of meaning.

Propositions and Attitudes: Russell's Neglected Insight

So far we have learned two lessons. First, truth conditions, no matter how fine-grained, are not enough. An adequate account of meaning and propositional attitudes requires structure-encoding propositions. Second, propositions of the traditional Frege-Russell sort lack the representational characteristics to do the job. No matter whether the constituents of propositions are Frege's mysterious "saturated" and "unsaturated" senses, or Russell's more tractable objects, properties, and propositional functions, propositions themselves are typically presented as merely formal constructions of some kind—tree structures, sequences, nested sets, etc.—involving those constituents. Since there is nothing intrinsically representational about these structures, they don't—in and of themselves—represent anything as being one way rather than another. Since it is only by being representational that anything becomes a candidate for being true or false, structured propositions of the familiar sort don't have truth conditions, on their own. We can, of course, *treat* them as objects to be interpreted. But if this just means *endowing them with meaning* in the way we endow formulas of an uninterpreted language with meaning—by using a truth theory to assign them truth conditions—then our account of the representational content of propositions will be little better than the failed theories of the truth conditions of sentences that pose as theories of their meanings. If progress is to be made, it must be made in some other way.

The key to making such progress is to recognize an inescapable fact: if the formal structures with which we might identify propositions aren't intrinsically representational, they can play a useful role in our theories only if their representational properties are somehow derived from the cognitive relations we bear to them. How might that be? Ironically, the classical text that does the most to help us answer this question is one that repudiates propositions altogether—namely, Russell's chapter, "Truth and Falsehood," in *The Problems of Philosophy*.[4] The propositions he there rejects are the structured complexes of objects and properties that he embraced eight years earlier in *Principles of Mathematics*. In *The Problems of Philosophy*, he offers his *multiple-relation theory of judgment* as a replacement for propositions as objects of the attitudes and bearers of truth value.

Russell's task there is to explain truth and falsity, and identify their bearers—subject to three self-imposed constraints: (i) truth

---

[4] Bertrand Russell, *The Problems of Philosophy* (New York: Oxford University Press, 1959); originally published in 1911.

bearers must be the sorts of things that can also be false, (ii) "if there were no beliefs, there could be no falsehood, and no truth either,"[5] and (iii) whether or not a belief is true must be an objective matter of fact, independent of us. He takes the first constraint to eliminate propositions as truth bearers, since, he thinks, any reasonable conception of their "unity" will make it impossible for them to be false.

> The necessity of allowing for falsehood makes it impossible to regard belief as a relation of the mind to a single object, which could be said to be what is believed. If belief were so regarded, we should find that, like acquaintance, it would not admit of the opposition of truth and falsehood, but would have to be always true. This may be made clear by examples. Othello believes falsely that Desdemona loves Cassio. We cannot say that this belief consists in a relation to a single object, [denoted by] 'Desdemona's love for Cassio', for if there were such an object, the belief would be true. There is in fact no such object, and therefore Othello can't have any relation to such an object. Hence his belief cannot possibly consist in a relation to this object.[6]

For Russell, propositions are complexes, the constituents of which are objects, properties, and relations, united, somehow, into a coherent whole. Thus, in order for there to be a proposition the constituents of which are Desdemona, loving, and Cassio (in that order), the relation of loving must somehow relate the other two. But for loving to do that is just for Desdemona to love Cassio—in

---

[5] Ibid., 120–21.
[6] Ibid., 124.

which case the complex *Desdemona's love for Cassio* will be a fact. In short, the unity required by the existence of the proposition that Desdemona loves Cassio requires it to be true. But that can't be right, for then there would be no false propositions.

This argument is Russell's 1911 response to the following worry expressed in his 1903 *Principles* (cited in chapter 2).

> Consider, for example, the proposition "A differs from B." The constituents of this proposition, if we analyze it, appear to be only A, difference, B. Yet these constituents, thus placed side by side, do not reconstitute the proposition. *The difference which occurs in the proposition actually relates A and B*, whereas the difference after analysis is a notion which has no connection with A and B.[7]

Before, he was willing to leave the unity of the proposition as an unexplained mystery, saying:

> A proposition, in fact, is essentially a unity, and when analysis has destroyed the unity, no enumeration of constituents will restore the proposition. The verb, when used as a verb, embodies the unity of the proposition, and is thus distinguishable from the verb considered as a term, though I do not know how to give a clear account of the precise nature of the distinction.[8]

By 1911 he had had enough of this mystery, as indicated by the passage immediately following the one from *The Problems of Philosophy* just quoted above.

---

[7] *Principles of Mathematics*, 49, my emphasis.
[8] *Principles of Mathematics*, 50.

It might be said that this belief is a relation to a different object namely [the object denoted by] 'that Desdemona loves Cassio'; but it is almost as difficult to suppose that there is such an object as this, when Desdemona does not love Cassio, as it was to suppose that there is [something denoted by] 'Desdemona's love for Cassio'. Hence it is better to seek for a theory of belief which does not make it consist in a relation of the mind to a single object.[9]

Russell's new alternative is to take the bearers of truth value to be entities he calls "beliefs"—meaning by this something other than *what one believes*—while taking believing, asserting, and other attitudes to be relations, not to objectively unified propositions, but to the very constituents that he had previously taken such propositions to mysteriously unify.

The relation involved in *judging* or *believing* must, if falsehood is to be duly allowed for, be taken to be a relation between several terms, not between two. When Othello believes that Desdemona loves Cassio, he must not have before his mind a single object, [denoted by] 'Desdemona's love for Cassio', or 'that Desdemona loves Cassio', for that would require that there should be objective falsehoods, which subsist independently of any minds. . . . Thus it is easier to account for falsehood if we take judgment to be a relation in which the mind and the various objects concerned all occur severally; that is to say, *Desdemona and loving and Cassio must all be terms in the relation which subsists when Othello believes that Desdemona loves Cassio*. This relation,

---

[9] *The Problems of Philosophy*, 124.

therefore, is a relation of four terms, since Othello also is one of the terms of the relation. . . . Thus *the actual occurrence, at the moment when Othello is entertaining his belief, is that the relation called 'believing' is knitting together into one complex whole* the four terms Othello, Desdemona, loving, and Cassio. What is called belief or judgment is nothing but this relation of believing or judging, which relates a mind to several things other than itself.[10]

Under the old analysis of propositional attitudes, 'Othello believes that Desdemona loves Cassio" reports a relation that holds between the believer, Othello, and that which he believes, namely, *that Desdemona loves Cassio.* However, since Desdemona doesn't, in fact, love Cassio, this requires the existence of a false proposition, which Russell rejects. Under his new analysis, the sentence reports a 4-place relation that unites Othello, the believer, with the several objects of his belief—Desdemona, the loving relation, and Cassio (in that order). Since Othello really does believe that Desdemona loves Cassio, the belief relation *really does relate* these objects—knitting them together into a complex entity, *Othello's belief that Desdemona loves Cassio,* which Russell takes to be a fact. If this belief were true, then one of its objects—the loving relation—would *really relate* the other two—Desdemona and Cassio (in that order)—knitting them together into a different complex entity, *Desdemona's love for Cassio,* which would itself be a fact. However, since Desdemona doesn't love Cassio, there is no such further fact, and the belief is false. The reason this isn't problematic for the new view is that in saying that *the belief is false* we are *not* saying that *what Othello believes* is false.

---

[10] Ibid., 125–26, my emphasis.

There is no such thing that he believes. Rather, we are saying that the fact that consists of *Othello's believing that Desdemona loves Cassio* is false. Since this complex entity, which Russell calls the "belief," really does exist, he takes his theory to have, at long last, successfully identified bearers of truth that can, unproblematically, also be bearers of falsity.

> We spoke of the relation called 'judging' or 'believing' as knitting together into one complex whole the subject and the objects. In this respect judging is exactly like every other relation. *Whenever a relation holds between two or more terms, it unites the terms into a complex whole.* If Othello loves Desdemona, there is such a complex whole as [that denoted by] 'Othello's love for Desdemona'. . . . *Whenever there is a relation which relates certain terms, there is a complex object formed of the union of those terms; and conversely, whenever there is a complex object, there is a relation which relates its constituents.* When an act of believing occurs, there is a complex, in which [that denoted by] 'believing' is the uniting relation, and subject and objects are arranged in a certain order by the 'sense' of the relation of believing. Among the objects, as we saw in considering 'Othello believes that Desdemona loves Cassio', one must be a relation—in this instance the relation [denoted by] 'loving'. But this relation, as it occurs in the act of believing, is not the relation which creates the unity of the complex whole consisting of the subject and the objects. The relation [denoted by] 'loving', *as it occurs in the act of believing, is one of the objects*—*it is a brick in the structure, not the cement.* The cement is the relation [denoted by] 'believing'. When the belief is true, there is another complex unity, in

which the relation which was one of the objects of the belief relates the other objects. Thus, e.g., if Othello believes truly that Desdemona loves Cassio, there is a complex unity, [denoted by] 'Desdemona's love for Cassio', which is composed exclusively of the objects of the belief, in the same order as they had in the belief, *with the relation which was one of the objects occurring now as the cement that binds together the other objects of belief.* On the other hand, when a belief is false, there is no such complex unity composed only of the objects of belief.[11]

That, in a nutshell, is Russell's multiple-relation theory of belief, and other attitudes. Unfortunately, there are several serious difficulties that render it inadequate. However, one of these difficulties points the way to reinstating propositions on a firmer foundation, as objects of the attitudes, and bearers of truth.

One set of difficulties stems from Russell's permissive and, I believe, overly optimistic attitude toward facts. Taking them to be really existing truth makers is bad enough.[12] Taking them also to be the bearers of truth and falsity is a further affront. Surely there are many truths, and also, one would hope, many falsehoods, that no one has ever believed. Russell's theory can't account for this, since in such cases, there will be no *facts that an agent believes so-and-so* with which to identify them. Even when agents do have the relevant beliefs, the identification of facts as bearers of truth value is problematic. On our ordinary conception of facts, talk of "true facts" is redundant at best, while talk of "false facts" is either

[11] Ibid., 127–28, my emphasis.
[12] For critical discussion, see Trenton Merricks, *Truth and Ontology* (Oxford: Oxford University Press, 2007); and Soames, "Truthmakers?," *Philosophical Books* 49 (2008), 317–27.

nonsensical, or something that requires interpretation. Yet for Russell, facts are precisely the things that are, literally, true or false.

The second set of problems concerns the ways in which the multiple-relation theory fails to capture the richness, variety, and utility of our ordinary talk of propositions and attitudes. At most, it offers a semantic analysis of attitude ascriptions of the form *x knows/believes/asserts (the proposition) that S*. However, the theory is silent about, and makes no provision for, talk of propositions outside of attitude ascriptions, or for attitude ascriptions in which the complement of the attitude verb is a name, singular definite description, or some other phrase or variable indicating quantification over propositions. Thus, the theory provides no analysis of examples like (5).

5a. Logicism is a thesis about the relationship between logic and mathematics.

 b. For every true proposition in the report, there are two other propositions in the report that are false.

 c. Bill asserted/denied Church's Thesis/Goldbach's Conjecture.

 d. Susan proved the proposition/several propositions that John denied.

 e. There are many propositions that no one has entertained, let alone proved or disproved.

The final problem with the theory is one that leads to a suggestion about how to transform it into a new and improved theory of propositions. It is a truism that a belief, assertion, hypothesis, or conjecture represents the world as being a certain way, and so is capable of being true or false. Ordinarily, what we mean by this is that *what is believed, asserted, hypothesized,* or *conjectured* represents the world, and so is true or false. Using the familiar name 'proposition' for these things, we may ask "*In virtue of what are propositions representational, and hence bearers of truth conditions?*" This was the key question about propositions that Frege and the early Russell weren't able to answer. Nevertheless, the problem is genuine. Surely, beliefs, assertions, hypotheses, and conjectures *are* representational. Hence, there should be an answer to the question of what makes them so. If Russell's multiple-relation theory is to have value, it must answer this question.

Fortunately, his theory does have value. However, bringing this out requires a little effort. As we have seen, according to the theory, beliefs, assertions, and the like are *facts* in which an agent is related by the relevant attitude relation (belief, assertion, etc.) to various objects, properties, and relations (which Russell calls objects of the agent's attitude). *To ask what makes all of these facts representational is to ask what the agent's cognitive attitude adds to the objects of his attitude to bring it about that the world is represented as being one way rather than another.* What, for example, does the agent add to the elements Desdemona, loving, and Cassio to bring it about that *the agent's belief that Desdemona loves Cassio* represents the world in the way that it does?

In asking this question, it is important to bear two points in mind. First, what one agent adds to these constituents to bring it about that his or her belief represents the world in this way is *the same* as what any other agent adds to bring it about that this other agent's belief represents the world in the same way. Second, what any agent adds to Desdemona, loving, and Cassio to bring it about that a *belief* that Desdemona loves Cassio represents the world in a certain way is *the same* as what an agent adds to those constituents to bring it about that an *assertion, hypothesis,* or *conjecture* that Desdemona loves Cassio represents things in the same way. When these two facts are kept in mind, the answer to our question is obvious. *What the agent does* in all these cases to bring it about that his or her belief, assertion, hypothesis, or conjecture *represents* Desdemona as loving Cassio is to *predicate* one constituent of the judgment—the loving relation—of the other two—Desdemona followed by Cassio.

This is the kernel of truth in Russell's multiple-relation theory. What unites the elements of a proposition, and gives it representational import, is something that agents do when they bear cognitive relations to it—namely, *predicate* one propositional constituent of the others. Since this is so no matter whether the representational content is believed, asserted, conjectured, hypothesized, or known, we can transform the multiple-relation theory back into a propositional theory by collecting the multiple constituents of all representationally equivalent instances of believing, asserting, and the like into a single formal structure in which one constituent is identified as predicated of the others. We may then give a deflationary account of what it is for an agent to bear the relation of *entertaining* (sometimes called "grasping") to this representational structure. It is simply for the agent to predicate that which is so indicated in the structure of the other constituents of the structure.

Other attitudes are parasitic on this. For one to bear the attitude of *believing* to a propositional structure p is to be disposed to endorse, accept, or subscribe to the predication needed to entertain p. Other attitudes follow in train. To know p is, to a first approximation, for p to be true, for one to believe p, and for one to be justified in so believing. To assert p is for one to commit oneself in conversation to treating p as if it were known.

In this way, we preserve the chief virtue of the multiple-relation theory—that of providing a plausible and unified story of how it is that beliefs, assertions, conjectures, and other attitudes are representational—while retaining a single set of objects for all the attitudes that preserves the utility and semantic richness of our ordinary talk of propositions.

For this to work, propositions must be bearers of truth value, as well as being objects of propositional attitudes. On this view, to say that what is believed is true is to say that a proposition is both believed and true. Suppose, for the sake of argument, that the proposition is identified with the elementary structure <the loving relation, <a,b>>. What is it for it to be true? Considered simply as a formal structure, this sequence of sequences is not representational at all, and so can't be true or false, on its own. According to our extension of the Russellian idea, ascriptions of truth conditions to it are relativized to certain attitudes we take toward it. In calling it true, or false, what we are saying is that it is true, or false, *when taken as it is, or would be, when entertained, believed, hypothesized, asserted, etc.—namely, as predicating loving of a and b, in that order.* In calling a more complex proposition p necessarily true (or false), we are saying that—when p is taken as it is, or would be, when entertained, asserted, etc.—it correctly (or incorrectly) describes what the universe would be like, no matter which metaphysically possible world-state obtained, or was instantiated.[13] For this to be so, it is not necessary for p to exist, or to be entertained, at every world-state. What is required is that the necessary and sufficient conditions for entertaining p not change from world-state to world-state, which they don't. It is

---

[13] This is only a rough, first approximation, to illustrate the general idea.

a contingent fact about us that we entertain various propositions, and in so doing predicate certain things of other things. However, it is part of what we mean by *entertaining* these structures that predicating certain things of other things is *necessary and sufficient* for entertaining them. This is why some propositions are true at world-states at which neither we, nor anyone else, entertains them. In the next chapter, I will explain this picture in greater detail.

Chapter 5

Toward a Theory of Propositions:
A Deflationary Account

IN CHAPTER 3, I argued that theories of meaning need propositions, which can't be sets of truth-supporting circumstances, but
rather must be complexes that encode the meanings of the constituents of the sentences that express them. In this chapter and
the next, I will sketch two ways of developing a theory of this
sort. In this chapter, I will develop a *deflationary* conception of
propositions, paying attention to the positive aspects of the view
which must be incorporated in any adequate theory of propositions. The chapter closes with a serious problem for the deflationary conception, which will pave the way for the development in
chapter 6 of a realist conception of propositions that builds on
the insights of the deflationary account.

The guiding idea behind the deflationary approach is that
propositions are structured complexes that are constructed out
of, or at least encode, the semantic contents of the constituents
of the sentences that express them. In illustrating this approach,
I will use a simple system of hierarchical (labeled) bracketing

to provide propositions in this sense. The idea is familiar from syntactic theories of natural language that take sentences (or their surface structures) to be phrase structure trees, with a root S-node dominating the nodes of its immediate constituents, which are further broken into subconstituents, until terminal nodes, occupied by lexical items, are reached. On the deflationary approach, the proposition expressed by a sentence is a hierarchical structure paralleling the syntactic structure of the sentence itself. The constituents of the proposition are the objects, properties, relations, and propositional functions that are, or encode, the meanings of the constituents of the sentence. For my purposes, the details of these structures won't matter. Nor will it matter that propositional structures may abstract away from some aspects of syntactic structure, resulting in a less than complete isomorphism between the two. Any abstract system will suffice for my purposes, as long as it is capable of marking all semantically significant distinctions found in the language for which the theory is constructed.

My discussion will focus on the structure of propositions. Whatever the right syntax for a given language turns out to be, all semantically significant aspects of syntactic structure must be encoded by the structured propositions expressed by its sentences. Of course, if there is one system of semantic structures meeting this condition, there will be many. For any unambiguous sentence S, each such system will identify a unique structure as *the proposition S expresses*. However, since several such systems may be equally good, there is a sense in which many different formal structures are good candidates for being that proposition. The situation is similar to one we face with natural numbers. Just as many appropriately ordered sequences of abstract objects of the right cardinality may play the role of natural numbers, so the elements of many systems of semantic structure may play the role of propositions expressed by sentences. Thus, we face the same problem, or pseudo-problem, of identifying the "real propositions" as we do in identifying the "real natural numbers."[1] I will return to this later. For now, I simply register my thought that we should be no more deterred by this problem from developing a systematic theory of propositions than we are deterred from developing arithmetical theories of the natural numbers.

I will use a variant of the predicate calculus, expanded to include modal operators and propositional attitude verbs to illustrate the view. I will take atomic formulas to follow the usual English subject-verb-object form in which the first argument of an n-place predicate precedes it. Truth-functional operators, (unrestricted) quantifiers, and modal operators will be given their usual treatment as expressions that combine with formulas to form formulas. Attitude verbs will be 2-place predicates the second arguments of which are the semantic contents of the sentences that follow them. The syntax of the language has been deliberately chosen to differ slightly from that of any version of the predicate calculus standardly in use. One reason for this is to make the language a bit more English-looking, but my main reason is to avoid misunderstanding, and to forestall premature disputes. Although the truth conditions assigned to sentences by the semantic theory I will sketch are completely standard, the fine structure of the propositions expressed reflects debatable options about what is predicated of what in nonatomic propositions. These choices have subtle consequences for the precise

---

[1] Paul Benacerraf, "What Numbers Cannot Be," *Philosophical Review* 74 (1965), 47–73.

characterization of the meanings of negations, conjunctions, quantifications, and other constructions—which will be addressed in chapter 7. The initial semantic system I will sketch is not meant to be a descriptively optimal account of any language now in use. Rather, it is an accurate account of a possible language—call it *PL*—that we could learn to speak. Learning how to construct and understand a semantic theory for it will, I hope, help us achieve similar results for actually spoken languages.

The structured propositions the theory assigns to formulas of PL share much of the structure of those formulas. Those involving quantifiers and lambda-abstracts are the chief exceptions. Here, I follow the well-trodden path of letting propositional functions play the role of (complex) properties. The property expressed by the predicate $\ulcorner \lambda v\ F(v) \urcorner$ is identified with the function g from an object o to the structured proposition expressed by F relative to an assignment of o to v. I will speak of this propositional function as being *predicated* of the object denoted by the argument of the lambda-predicate—where, by predicating g of an object, I mean predicating *the property of being something to which g assigns a true proposition*, of that object.

Whenever two formulas express structurally different propositions (relative to assignments of values to variables), both the propositional functions gotten by attaching lambda-operators to the formulas, and the properties of being objects to which those functions assign truths, will be different—even if the formulas themselves are logically equivalent. In virtue of this, the semantic content of a lambda-predicate *encodes* (rather than shares) the syntactic structure of the formula used to construct it. A similar point holds for semantic contents of quantified formulas. The proposition expressed by such a formula predicates the higher-order property expressed by the quantifier, not of a content that shares its structure with that of the matrix formula, but of the *propositional function* expressed by the lambda-version of that formula. Although other treatments of the semantic contents of quantification and lambda-abstraction are possible, this one is both simple and familiar, and so will serve my purposes. In chapter 7—after I have used the system to illustrate my foundational view of propositions, and their role in theories of meaning—I will return to quantification, and other constructions, to discuss various difficulties and complications involving them.

Structured propositions are assigned to sentences of PL as follows:

a. The proposition expressed by an atomic formula $[_S [_{NP} t_1]$ $[_{VP} [_V P] [_{NP} t_2] \ldots [_{NP} t_n]]]$ relative to an assignment A is the structure $[_{Prop} [_{Arg} o_1] [_{Pred} P^*] [_{Arg} o_2] \ldots [_{Arg} o_n]]$, where P^* is the property expressed by P, and o_i is the referent of t_i relative to A. The structured proposition is also represented by the following tree: [2]

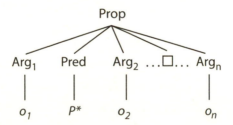

b. The proposition expressed by a formula $[_S[_{NP} t] [_{VP}[_V \lambda vF(v)]]]$ relative to A is $[_{Prop} [_{Arg} o] [_{Pred} g]]$, where o is the referent of t relative to A, and g is the function from

[2] In the interest of simplicity, I have abstracted away from the syntactic structure of the VP-node in the atomic formula, producing a flat propositional structure. This isn't essential, as the extra structure of the formula could easily be built into the proposition. However, failure to do so isn't disqualifying, and is meant to illustrate the point that complete isomorphism between syntactic and semantic structure isn't required.

individuals o′ to propositions expressed by F(v) relative to an assignment A′ that assigns o′ as the referent
of v, and otherwise agrees with A. As before, the structured proposition can be represented as a tree.

c.   The propositions expressed by negations $[_S[_{SOP} \sim][_S P]]$
and conjunctions $[_S[_S P] [_{SOP} \&] [_S Q]]$ relative to A are
$[_{Prop} [_{Pred} NEG] [_{Arg} Prop P]]$ and $[_{Prop} [_{Arg} Prop P] [_{Pred}$
CONJ] $[_{Arg} Prop Q]]$, respectively, where Prop P and
Prop Q are the propositions expressed by P and Q relative to A, NEG is the property *being not true*, and CONJ
is the property *being jointly true*. The corresponding
trees are:

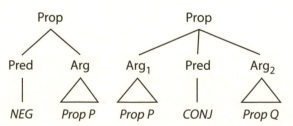

Other truth-functional compounds (disjunction, material conditionals and biconditionals) are treated
similarly.[3]

---

[3] For the sake of familiarity, I let the property NEG precede its argument, similarly for
the properties NEC and POSS of *being necessarily true* and *being possibly true* covered in
clause (d).

d. The proposition expressed by the modal formula $[_S[_{SOP}$
NEC] $[_S$ P]] is $[_{Prop}[_{Pred}$ NEC] $[_{Arg}$ Prop P]], where NEC
is the property of *being necessarily true*—similarly for
the possibility operator. The corresponding trees are:

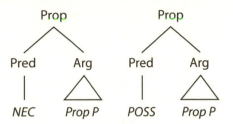

e. The proposition expressed by the quantified formula
$[_S[_{Quant} \exists v]\ [_S$ P]] relative to A is $[_{Prop}\ [_{Arg}$ g] $[_{Pred}$ SOME]],
where SOME is the property *being sometimes true*—
i.e., of being a function that assigns a true proposition
to some object, and g is as in (b). The story is the same
for formulas involving the universal quantifier, except
that the property expressed by the quantifier is *being
always true*—i.e., assigning a true proposition to every
object.

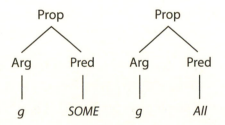

f. The proposition expressed by a belief ascription $[_S[_{NP}$ t]
$[_{VP}\ [_V$ believes] $[_{Arg}[_{AOP}$ that] $[_S$ P]]]] relative to A is $[_{Prop}$
$[_{Arg}$ o] $[_{Pred}$ BELIEVE] $[_{Arg}$ Prop P]], where BELIEVE is
the belief relation, o is the referent of t relative to A,
Prop P is the proposition expressed by P relative to A,

and 'that' forms a singular term directly referring to Prop P (similarly for other attitude ascriptions).

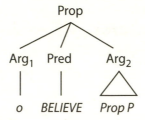

The truth conditions of sentences of PL are derived from the truth conditions of the propositions they express: S is true iff the proposition it expresses is true. The truth conditions of propositions are determined as follows.

a.   A proposition $[_{Prop}[_{Arg} o_1][_{Pred} P^*][_{Arg} o_2] \ldots [_{Arg} o_n]]$ is true at a world-state w iff the property P^* predicated of $<o_1 \ldots o_n>$ is true of those arguments at w.

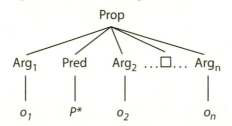

b.   A proposition $[_{Prop} [_{Arg} o] [_{Pred} g]]$ is true at w iff g(o) is true at w iff the property *being something to which g assigns a true proposition*, predicated of o, is true of o at w.

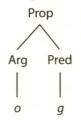

c.   A proposition $[_{Prop}[_{Pred}NEG][_{Arg}Prop\ P]]$ is true at w iff
the property *not being true* predicated of Prop P is true
of it at w iff Prop P is false at w; $[_{Prop}[_{Arg}Prop\ P]\ [_{Pred}$
CONJ] $[_{Arg}Prop\ Q]]$ is true at w iff the relation *being
jointly true* predicated of Prop P and Prop Q is true of
them at w iff both Prop P and Prop Q are true at w.

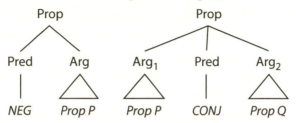

d.   A proposition $[_{Prop}[_{Pred}\ NEC][_{Arg}\ Prop\ P]]$ is true at w iff
the property *being necessarily true* predicated of Prop
P is true of it at w iff Prop P is true at all world-states
possible from w. $[_{Prop}[_{Pred}\ POSS]\ [_{Arg}\ Prop\ P]]$ is true at
w iff the property *being possibly true* predicated of Prop
P is true of it at w iff Prop P is true at some world-state
possible from w.

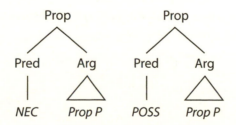

e. $[_{Prop}[_{Arg}\ g][_{Pred}SOME]]$ is true at w iff the property *being
sometimes true,* predicated of g, is true of g at w iff for
some o, g(o) is true at w. $[_{Prop}[_{Arg}\ g]\ [_{Pred}ALL]]$ is true at
w iff the property *being always true,* predicated of g, is
true of g at w iff for all o, g(o) is true at w.

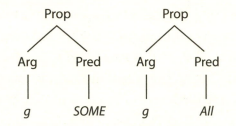

f.   A proposition [_Prop_[_Arg_ o] [_Pred_ BELIEVE][_Arg_ Prop P]] is
     true at w iff the belief relation predicated of the pair o,
     Prop P is true of them at w iff at w, o believes Prop P.

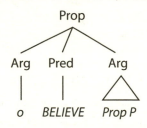

The truth conditions assigned to belief ascriptions like (1) are
especially interesting.

1.   'John believes that ∃x (x loves Mary)' is true at w iff at
     w, John believes the proposition [_Prop_[_Arg_ g][_Pred_ SOME]],
     in which the property *being a propositional function
     that assigns a truth to some object* is predicated of the
     function g that assigns to an individual o the proposi-
     tion [_Prop_[_Arg_ o][_Pred_ the loving relation][_Arg_ Mary]] that
     predicates the loving relation of the pair o, Mary.

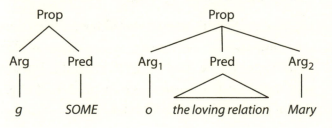

In chapter 3, I gave a similar statement of the truth conditions of this sentence using a theory that took propositions to be ordered n-tuples. There, I argued that the resulting T-sentence didn't provide informative truth conditions because we couldn't read enough information off the bare n-tuple with which the object of belief was identified to ascertain its content. At best we could use an assignment of truth conditions to that n-tuple to locate the object of John's belief as being somewhere in a class of propositions necessarily, and apriori, equivalent to the proposition that someone loves Mary. If the new account is to work, it must do better than that. It does. Theorem (1) tells us that the proposition John believes predicates *being sometimes true* of the function that assigns an arbitrary individual o the proposition that predicates the loving relation of the pair <o, Mary>—which is just a round-about way of saying that the proposition John believes predicates *being instantiated* of the property *loving Mary*. Since this is a paraphrase of the claim that some individual loves Mary, which is what the complement clause '∃x (x loves Mary)' of the belief-ascribing sentence intuitively means, we can read off what the belief ascription means from the proposition assigned to it. This is how a semantic theory that assigns structured propositions to sentences ought to work.

The key to this result is the inclusion of information about what is predicated of what in structured propositions. But, one might object, isn't this too easy? Even bare n-tuples of objects and properties can, *if one so stipulates*, be interpreted so that information about what is to be predicated of what may be read off the positions of items in an n-tuple. Surely, the objector maintains, there is no substantive difference between such a strategy, and one that uses mnemonic labels like 'Prop', 'Pred', 'Arg' to indicate what is predicated of what. In both cases the needed information comes from stipulation or interpretation.

Although this point is correct, it need not be an objection. We know from our experience of language that we can use *sentences* to predicate some things of other things. When we do, certain abstract objects—expression types—are predicated of things designated by other expressions in the sentence. We recognize the expressions to be predicated by their lexical identity and their position in syntactic structure. However, there is nothing *intrinsic* to the identity of a lexical item, thought of as a collection of syntactic and phonological features, or to its position in the hierarchical structure of a sentence S, that determines that an utterance of S is understood as predicating that item of something. At bottom what determines that which S predicates, as well as that of which it is predicated, is how S is understood by speakers-hearers. In short, the representational content of sentences is due to our cognitive attitudes toward them. Since we have no clue about how any abstract object could have representational content apart from such attitudes, a similar approach must be taken to the representational content of propositions, if they are to figure in our theories.

What are the relevant cognitive attitudes we bear to propositions? It is tempting to appeal to those, like assertion, that are mediated by our relations to sentences that express them. Although there is something to this idea, it can't be the last word. For one thing, some propositions aren't expressed by any public-language sentences. For another, some propositional attitudes aren't linguistically mediated at all. Nor will it do to postulate an unconsciously utilized "language of human thought" to accommodate such cases. In addition to being little more than unsupported speculation, such a postulation is not adequate to the task. There is nothing in our notions of knowledge, belief, and other cognitive attitudes that restricts them to human agents. Since all these attitudes are relations to propositions, neither the attitudes that possible agents bear to propositions, nor the representational nature of those propositions themselves, can require all attitude-bearing agents to share any supposed species-wide "language of thought" specific to human beings.

To get a grip on propositions we need to start at a more basic cognitive level. What is it to entertain a proposition? It is, I suggest, to predicate something of something else. To entertain the proposition *that o is red* is to predicate redness of o. Although predication is, like negation, a primitive notion, it is easily illustrated. When we see an object o *as red*, we predicate redness of it. It is in virtue of this that our perceptual experience represents o as *being red*, which is one way of entertaining the proposition *that o is red*. We also predicate redness of o, and hence entertain this proposition, when we form the nonlinguistic perceptual *belief* that o is red. We do the same when we understand an utterance of 'This is red', while taking the predicate to express the property *being red* and the subject to refer to o. These are three ways of predicating redness of o, and hence of entertaining the proposition *that o is red*.

The next step in the argument is crucial for the deflationary theory of propositions. One might grant that predicating redness of o is necessary and sufficient for one to entertain the proposition *that o is red*, and that one may do this in each of the ways I have sketched. Still, one might wonder what this has to do with entertaining the constituent structure tree (2), which the semantic theory for PL assigns to the sentence 'O is red'.

2.   [$_{Prop}$ [$_{Arg}$ o] [$_{Pred}$ Redness]]

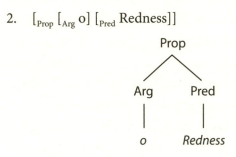

Structures like (2), which are assigned to sentences, are the theorist's creations. The theorist *stipulates* that to entertain (2) is to predicate redness of o. In saying this he is, in effect, assigning a new, technical meaning to the verb 'entertain' that explains what is meant by the theoretical claim that an agent entertains one of his abstract structures. Next, the theorist offers the bridge principle (3a), which relates that theoretical claim, on the right side of the biconditional, to the empirical claim on the left.

3a.   An agent entertains the proposition that o is red iff the agent entertains (2).

A similar strategy is used for every propositional attitude.

Since to entertain the proposition *that o is red* is simply to predicate redness of o, and since this predication is included in every attitude with that content, entertaining the proposition is one component of any propositional attitude we bear to it. To *judge* that o is red is to predicate redness of o, while endorsing that predication. To *believe* that o is red is, roughly, to be disposed to judge that o is red. To *know* that o is red is (roughly) to believe that o is red, while being justified in so doing (in a case in which o is red). To *assert* that o is red is, essentially, to make a conversational commitment, by assertively uttering something, to treat the proposition *that o is red* as something one knows. Given these characterizations, the theorist adds (3b–d) to (3a), thereby generating testable empirical predictions that connect the theoretical claims made by the semantic or cognitive theory, including those on the right of 'iff', with the ordinary claims on the left.

3b.   An agent believes the proposition that o is red iff the agent believes (2).

  c.   An agent knows that o is red iff the agent knows (2).

  d.   An agent asserts that o is red iff the agent asserts (2).

Since the hierarchical structure of the proposition (2) is essentially the same as the syntactic structure of the sentence 'O is red' that expresses it, one way of entertaining it is to understand an isomorphic linguistic structure that expresses it. However, one can also entertain it without the help of any linguistic, or other abstract, intermediary—as we do in perceptual experience, and nonlinguistic belief. It is even possible to entertain (2) by understanding a different, co-contentful utterance the syntactic structure of which differs in some respects from that of 'O is red'. This point generalizes to other sentences and propositions.

Having explained what it is to entertain an *atomic proposition*, we next must specify what it is to entertain nonatomic propositions. First consider negations. To entertain the proposition expressed by the negation of the sentence 'O is red' is, first, to predicate redness of o, and thereby to entertain (2), and, then to predicate *not being true* of it, and hence to entertain (4) (which, by an extension of (3a), is to entertain the proposition *that it is not the case that o is red*).

4. $[_{\text{Prop}}[_{\text{Pred}} \text{NEG}][_{\text{Arg}} [_{\text{Prop}} [_{\text{Arg}} \text{o}] [_{\text{Pred}} \text{Redness}]]]]$

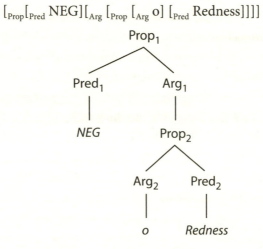

For now, I will take this proposition to be identical with the proposition *that o isn't red*, while also taking negation in PL to be the same as negation in English. Similar assumptions will be made about the relationship between other sentence-forming constructions in PL and those in English. In chapter 7, I will take up the question of whether the relationship between English and PL may be more complicated.

Next consider conjunctions. To entertain the proposition expressed by 'O is red & O* is circular' is (a) to predicate redness of o (and so to entertain (2)), (b) to predicate circularity of o*, and so to entertain (5),

5. $[_{\text{Prop}} [_{\text{Arg}} \text{o}^*] [_{\text{Pred}} \text{Circularity}]]$

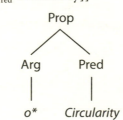

and (c) to predicate *being true* of both, and thereby to entertain (6) (which, for now, we identify with the proposition *that o is red and o* is circular*).

6. $[_{Prop} [_{Arg} [_{Prop} [_{Arg} o] [_{Pred} Redness]]] [_{Pred} CONJ] [_{Arg} [_{Prop}$
     $[_{Arg} o^*] [_{Pred} Circularity]]]]$

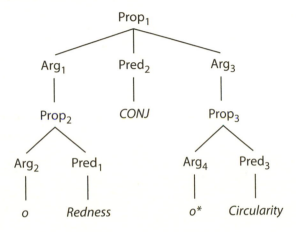

To entertain (6) it is necessary and sufficient to make the predications (a), (b), and (c) *and only these*. Since to entertain the conjunction of this proposition with, e.g., the proposition *that 1 = 1* is to make further predications as well, entertaining the original proposition doesn't involve entertaining the latter, trivially equivalent, proposition—which is as it should be given the different structure and constituents of the two propositions. In this way, the theory avoids the routine closure of propositional attitudes under trivial necessary and apriori equivalence that is the bane of all attempts to identify propositions with sets of truth-supporting circumstances.

Entertaining modal propositions follows the same pattern. To entertain (7)

7. $[_{Prop}[_{Pred}\text{NEC}]\ [_{Arg}[_{Prop}[_{Arg}[_{Prop}[_{Arg}\ o]\ [_{Pred}\ \text{Redness}]]]\ [_{Pred}$
$\text{COND}]\ [_{Arg}[_{Prop}[_{Arg}\ o]\ [_{Pred}\ \text{Colored}]]]]]]]$

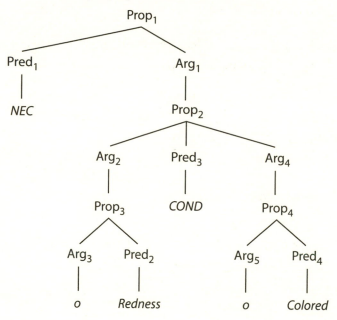

is to entertain the proposition *that if o is red, then o is colored*, and to predicate the property *being necessarily true* of it, thereby entertaining the proposition *that it is a necessary truth that if o is red, then o is colored*. Entertaining belief ascriptions is similar. To entertain the proposition

8. $[_{Prop}[_{Arg}\ \text{John}]\ [_{Pred}\ \text{BELIEVE}]\ [_{Arg}\ [_{Prop}\ [_{Arg}\ o]\ [_{Pred}$
$\text{Redness}]]]]$

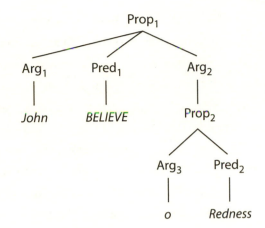

is to entertain the proposition *that o is red*, and to predicate the belief relation of the pair of which it is the second member and John is the first, thereby entertaining the proposition *that John believes that o is red*.

The semantics of PL assumes the Frege-Russell account of quantification according to which the sentence (9a) expresses the proposition (9b).

9a.   ∃x x is red.

9b.   [$_{Prop}$ [$_{Arg}$ g] [$_{Pred}$ SOME]]

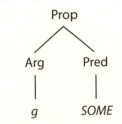

To entertain (9b) is to predicate *being a function that maps at least one object onto a truth* of the function that maps o onto proposition (2). But for the convenience of using propositional functions in place of properties, this is just to entertain the proposition *that redness is true of at least one thing,* which is the Frege-Russell version of the proposition *that something is red.*

Each of these explanations of what it is to entertain a *non-atomic proposition* relies on the legitimacy of ascribing truth to propositions. This may seem unproblematic, since our semantic theory for PL has rules that recursively assign them truth conditions. However, the ability to write such rules means nothing, unless one can justify the claim that the things to which they apply are genuinely representational, and so truth-apt. Propositions, as here understood, are abstract, hierarchical structures the ultimate constituents of which are individuals, properties, and propositional functions. Although this doesn't prevent them from being representational, nothing intrinsic to their structure or constituents makes them so. Rather, they are representational only in virtue of the cognitive attitudes one may bear to them. What makes the structure (2) represent o as red is that predicating its Pred-constituent of its Arg-constituent is necessary and sufficient for entertaining it. It is in virtue of this that we speak of the structure (2) as itself predicating redness of o. Since a proposition that does this, and makes no further predication, is true iff o is red, the truth conditions of (2) are derived from what it predicates of what. The point generalizes to other, atomic and nonatomic, propositions.

On this picture, neither the truth of a proposition nor that of a sentence requires anyone to have ever entertained it. What is required is that ascriptions of truth value be relativized to the way in which the truth-bearer is taken. Ascriptions of truth value to the hierarchical structures that are sentences are relativized to how those sentences are *understood* by speakers. Ascriptions of truth values to the hierarchical structures that are propositions are relativized to what is required to *entertain* them, which, in the case of (2), involves predicating redness of o.

This brings out an important difference in the ways in which the representational contents of sentences and propositions are tied to cognitive attitudes of agents. Whereas the existence and representational contents of sentences depend on speakers who *endow* them with contents, the existence and representational contents of propositions are not similarly contingent on agents. No one in the age of the dinosaurs understood any English sentences, or used them to mean anything. Thus, it is plausible to suppose that there was neither an English language nor any contentful English sentence then. The same is true of possible world-states at which there are no language users, which is why the claim expressed by (10) is false when evaluated at such a world-state.[4]

10. 'Snow is white' is a true sentence of English iff snow is white.

By contrast, (11a)—which can be taken as ascribing truth conditions to (11b)—is true at every possible world-state.

---

[4] Although (10) is false when evaluated at a world-state w at which snow is white but there are no English sentences, (10*) is true.

(10*) 'Snow is white' is *true at w* iff snow is white at w.

A sentence S has the relational property of *being true at w* iff what we use S to express here and now is a true description of what the universe would be like if w were to obtain. By contrast, at w, S has the monadic property of *being true* iff at w speakers use S to say something true. The contrast between S's *being true at w* and its being such, at w, that S *is true*, parallels the contrast, explained on pp. 345–46 of *Philosophical Analysis in the Twentieth Century*, vol. 2, between 'Aristotle' *referring at w* to Aristotle and it's being such, at w, that 'Aristotle' *refers* to Aristotle.

11a.   The proposition that snow is white is true iff snow
is white.

b.   [_{Prop} [_{Arg} snow] [_{Pred} Whiteness]]

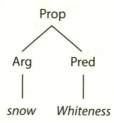

The truth of (11b) at a world-state w depends solely on the fact
that (11b) predicates whiteness of snow, which in turn depends
solely on the fact that it is necessary and sufficient for (11b) to be
entertained at any world-state that some agent predicates whiteness of snow at that world-state. If no agent does this, then (11b)
won't be *entertained* at w. However it will remain *entertainable*
there. Since the necessary and sufficient conditions for entertaining (11b) don't change from one world-state to another, it predicates whiteness of snow at every world-state, and hence bears its
truth conditions essentially. At world-states at which some agents
see snow *as white,* or form the nonlinguistic perceptual belief *that
snow is white,* (11b) will be entertained, even if it is not linguistically expressed. At world-states devoid of cognitive agents, it will
still be entertainable, and hence representational, even though no
one entertains it.

Does it seem strange that the truth conditions of propositions
are, in this way, *essential,* even though they are not *intrinsic*? If so,
perhaps it is because one is thinking about entertaining a proposition incorrectly. If, outside of the present discussion, I were to
draw the structure (11b) on the blackboard, indicating that its

terminal nodes were occupied by the kind snow and the property whiteness, one who saw and understood me would, thereby, bear a cognitive attitude to (11b), and so become acquainted with it in a certain way. However, one would not count as *entertaining* it, in the sense discussed here, if one didn't *interpret* it by predicating whiteness of snow—which one needn't do in the situation imagined. One's cognitive encounter would fully reveal the structure and constituents of (11b), without carrying information about representational content. When the structure is thought of in this way, it is evident that its content isn't intrinsic to it, but rather must be due to some use to which it is put.

This use comes from the role structured propositions play in our theories—as a measure of cognitive states in which agents predicate properties of things. In physical theory we use numbers, and other abstract objects, to talk about theoretically significant relations that physical magnitudes of various sorts bear to one another. In semantic and psychological theory we use abstract propositional structures to talk about theoretically significant relations that representational cognitive states and activities bear to one another, and to the world. The conditions the theory specifies as necessary and sufficient for *entertaining* these propositional structures are what allow us to use them to track the relationships that hold among actual and possible predications by agents. This provides us with the sense in which the truth conditions of propositions are essential to them. What is essential to the use to which we put propositions is the range of actual and possible predications they track. Since predications are essentially representational, that which tracks them must also be.

The analogy between the role of one system of abstract objects—numbers—in our physical theories, and the role of another system of abstract objects—propositions—in our psychological and linguistic theories, brings with it a version of the *Benacerraf point*. Just as the members of any appropriately ordered set of the right cardinality can play the role of the natural numbers, so the members of any set of abstract objects capable of encoding all the predications needed to give a semantic theory for a language can play the role of the propositions expressed in that language. Just as any such choice for the numbers will preserve all the arithmetical theorems, so any corresponding choice for the propositions will preserve the semantic theorems.

Recall theorem (1) discussed above.

1.   'John believes that $\exists x$ (x loves Mary)' is true at w iff at w, John believes the proposition $[_{\text{Prop}}[_{\text{Arg}}$ g$][_{\text{Pred}}$ SOME$]]$, in which the property *being a propositional function that assigns a truth to some object* is predicated of the function g that assigns to an individual o the proposition $[_{\text{Prop}}[_{\text{Arg}}$ o$][_{\text{Pred}}$ the loving relation$][_{\text{Arg}}$ Mary$]]$ that predicates the loving relation of the pair o, Mary.

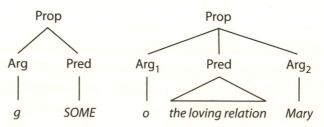

This theorem tells us that the belief ascription is true iff John believes something that predicates *being a propositional function that assigns a truth to some object* of the function that assigns o a proposition that predicates the loving relation of <o, Mary> (and which doesn't predicate anything further of anything else). In so doing, the theorem provides us with the information that John believes that *loving Mary* is true of someone. In relying on (1), we make use of one particular abstract structure, as that expressed by the complement clause of the belief ascription. However, we could have made other choices. Since different systems of abstract structures can play the role of propositions in our theories, variants of (1) involving those structures are possible. Since they all carry the same information about the agent's predications, they can all be accepted as true.

Putting n such variants together, we will get (1_n), where the P_is are different abstract structures chosen by the different variants of the semantic theory to play the role of the proposition expressed by the complement clause of the belief ascription.

1_n. The sentence 'John believes that $\exists x$ (x loves Mary)' is true at w iff at w, John believes P_1 iff at w, John believes P_2 iff . . . iff at w, John believes P_n.

This claim isn't relativized to any one version of the semantics, but comes from simultaneously accepting all of them. Since there seems to be nothing to prevent us from doing this, there seems to be nothing to prevent us from taking (1_n) to be true. Of course, if we do, then we aren't going to be able to answer the question, *"Which structure, really, is the proposition that $\exists x$ (x loves Mary)?"* The inability to do so is something the proponent of the deflationary conception of propositions must be prepared to accept— perhaps with the declaration that the question has no answer.

This position is different from the one taken by Benacerraf in response to the corresponding question about which sets natural numbers really are. He holds that numbers can't really be sets at all, because there are too many different sets that each number could equally well be taken to be. Rather, he argues, numbers are *sui generis*—not to be reduced to, or identified with, anything else. For the propositional deflationist, the corresponding position about propositions is a nonstarter. To take propositions to be *sui generis* is to take them to be abstract objects that are *intrinsically* representational, and hence bearers of truth value. For this to be so, they would have to somehow predicate certain things of other things, entirely on their own, independent of any cognitive attitudes agents bear to them. Since we have no idea how to make sense of this, we shouldn't accept it.

For the deflationist, propositions are theoretical constructs used to track the predications that make up the cognitive lives of agents. Although these constructs have truth conditions, their truth conditions are not intrinsic to them, but arise from a kind of convention. For an abstract structure, identified as a proposition, to have truth conditions is for it to be taken in the way required for one to bear the special attitude of entertaining to it. Since predicating redness of o is necessary and sufficient for one to count as entertaining the abstract structure (2), we assign (2) the condition of being true iff o is red, *relative to this way of being related to it.* Its truth conditions depend on what it would take for an agent to entertain it, even though it is not *endowed* with representational content by agents in the way that sentences of a language are.

At this point, one may worry about the legitimacy of characterizing propositions—thought of as theoretically useful tracking devices—as representational in virtue of what may seem to be an artificial relation they bear to the predicative acts of agents. The worry is that propositions in this sense are nothing more than theoretically useful fictions. Since, on this view, the only things there *really* are in the world are the cognitive states and activities being measured, it *is* false that there are nonlinguistic, abstract structures of the sort discussed here that are bearers of truth value and objects of the attitudes.

Although I am not sure there is any obvious way of establishing this negative conclusion, there is a result in the neighborhood that is genuinely worrying. The artificial language PL used to illustrate the deflationary theory of propositions was designed with a particular feature in mind: the only proposition-forming operation it employs is predication.

(i)   Propositions expressed by atomic formulas are formed by predicating properties of objects.

(ii) Propositions expressed by quantified sentences are formed by predicating higher-order properties of propositional functions, which play the role of properties expressed by the formulas to which quantifiers are attached.

(iii) Propositions expressed by truth-functionally compound sentences are formed by predicating truth or falsity of their constituent propositions.

(iv) Propositions expressed by attitude ascriptions are formed by predicating an attitude relation of an agent and a proposition.

(v)   Modal propositions are formed by predicating *being necessarily true,* or *being possibly true,* of propositions.

If the theory is to work, all proposition-forming predications must be predications that agents can perform. How are they able to do so? In the case of predications forming atomic propositions, the answer seems obvious. Agents are capable of performing these predications by virtue of having both the properties to be predicated, and the objects of which they are predicated, some-how in mind. The same can be said of cases in which higher-order properties are predicated of lower-order properties or propositional functions to form quantified propositions. Agents perform the predications because they have both the properties predicated, and that of which they are predicated, in mind. Since all other, compound, propositions expressed by sentences of PL are formed by predicating properties of simpler propositions, the same result should apply to them. *In order to entertain any of these compound propositions, agents must have their constituent propositions in mind.*

Is there a plausible explanation of how they do this? Consider negation, which is the simplest case. To entertain the negation of the proposition *that o is red*, one first predicates redness of o, and then, in effect, says to oneself *"that's not true,"* referring to the result of one's initial predication. What is this result? According to the theory, it must be the proposition *that o is red.* But if asked to identify this proposition with an abstract structure, the defla-tionist will tell us that there are many equally good candidates, no one of which is better than the others. Although the agent has predicated untruth of one, and only one, proposition, no identification of that proposition with any abstract structure is determinately correct. For many structures, the identification is determinately false; for others it has no determinate truth value. So, we are left with the idea that agents implicitly refer to unique propositions that they have in mind when predicating properties of them, even though it is impossible to determinately identify the subjects of those predications.

This is troubling. How can one say both (i) that there is one and only one proposition—the proposition *that o is red*—which the agent has both picked out and predicated untruth of, and (ii) that for every entity x, it is not determinately true that the agent has picked out, and predicated untruth of, x? There are super-valuationist treatments of indeterminacy, and truth value gaps, according to which pairs of claims like this *are* jointly true—e.g., the claim (i) that there *is* a precise number n of seconds such that a man is young iff he has lived less than n seconds, and the claim (ii) that for any number n, it is *not determinately true* that a man is young iff he has lived less than n seconds. Though I am deeply skeptical about such accounts of sorites examples, I have held open the possibility that supervaluationism might play a role in other cases—e.g., those in which an agent seems to have asserted some proposition or other, within a limited range, even though for each candidate proposition p it is indeterminate that the agent asserted p.[5] If that is really a genuine possibility, then perhaps the deflationary theory of propositions can be defended along similar lines. However, it is not obvious that it can—because it is not obvious that agents can correctly be said to have *any* of the theorist's abstract structures in mind in a sense sufficiently robust to make them the targets of the agents' acts of predication. Since these structures must be predication targets, if the deflationist's account of entertaining compound propositions by predicating properties of their constituents is to be viable, this worry strikes at the heart of the deflationary theory of propositions.

The theory's motivating idea is that propositions are construc-tions used by theorists to model the structure of agents' acts of predication. However, since the acts being modeled include those

---

[5] See pp. 371–72 of my "The Possibility of Partial Definition," in *Philosophical Essays*, vol. 2.

in which properties are predicated of *propositions*, it would seem that propositions must be parts of the reality being modeled, rather than merely components of the model. This challenges the theory's leading idea. Whether or not it *refutes* the theory may be contestable. However, it does raise a serious doubt about it. Instead of trying to reconcile ourselves to this doubt, we are, I believe, better advised to try to incorporate the insights of the deflationary account into a realist theory of propositions for which this doubt doesn't arise.[6]

---

[6] Thanks to an anonymous referee for a useful suggestion about this final paragraph.

Chapter 6

The Cognitive-Realist Theory of Propositions

I BEGIN WITH an insightful suggestion I owe to James Pryor. Since propositions are theoretical devices for tracking acts of predication by agents, why not take them to be *act types*, rather than the abstract structures with which the deflationist identifies them? On this proposal, the proposition that snow is white is identified, not with the tree structure

1. $[_{\text{Prop}} [_{\text{Arg}} \text{snow}] [_{\text{Pred}} \text{Whiteness}]]$

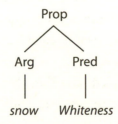

but with the act type *predicating whiteness of snow*. This idea has three main virtues. First, propositions, so conceived, are intrinsically connected to the cognitive acts they are needed to track. Second, in identifying the proposition *that o is F* with the act type *predicating Fness of o*, rather than with any particular event in which that act is performed, we provide an object to which all agents who entertain the proposition bear the same relation.[1] Finally, the proposal makes a plausible claim about what propositions *really are*, rather than merely choosing abstract structures, about which there is bound to be some arbitrariness, to *play the role of propositions*.

Despite these virtues, there are serious worries to be addressed. The first involves predication, and the role it plays in justifying the idea that propositions represent things as being certain ways. According to the deflationist, propositions predicate some things of other things (by virtue of the fact that these predications are necessary and sufficient to entertain them). For example, the proposition *that snow is white* predicates whiteness of snow, and thereby represents snow as white. By contrast, the act type of predicating one thing of another doesn't itself predicate anything of anything. Just as the act type of kissing Martha doesn't kiss Martha, so the act type of predicating whiteness of snow doesn't predicate whiteness of snow. Thus, if an entity can represent something as being one way rather than another only if it predicates something of that thing, then act types aren't representational—and so can't be propositions.

But is it true that an entity can represent something as being a certain way only if it predicates something of that thing? Think of sentences. The sentence 'Snow is white' is commonly said to represent snow as being white, and even to predicate whiteness of snow. But what this comes to is simply that *speakers* use the

---

[1] Here, and throughout this chapter, I use 'F' as a schematic letter, rather than a metalinguistic variable.

sentence to predicate whiteness of snow. The sense in which *a sentence* predicates a property P of something A is that of being a structure in which an expression corresponding to P occupies the place reserved for specifying that which *speakers* predicate, while an expression corresponding to A occupies the place reserved for specifying what they predicate it of. Thus, the sentence 'Snow is white' doesn't literally, or intrinsically, predicate whiteness of snow, any more than the abstract structure (1) does.

Could something similar be said about act types? They don't literally predicate anything of anything either, although agents who perform them do. Just as there is a *derivative* sense in which sentences predicate properties of things, because their speakers do, so, it might be argued, there is a *derivative* sense in which the act type *predicating P of A* predicates P of A in virtue of the fact that one who performs the act does. Thus, it might be thought, truth conditions can be ascribed to act types, just as they are to sentences, in which case act types might qualify as propositions after all.

Although this is, I think, the best case that can be made for taking propositions to be acts of predication, it doesn't seem to be quite good enough. That it isn't is signaled by the fact that ascriptions to propositions of *what can be said of act types*, as well as ascriptions to act types of *what can be said of propositions*, strike us as bizarre, or incoherent. Whereas it is perfectly coherent to say that predicating brilliance of John is what I just did, or that the proposition that John is brilliant is false, it would be incoherent to say "**The proposition that John is brilliant is what I just did*," or "**What I plan to do* (when I plan to predicate brilliance of John) *is false*." Moreover, although it is correct to say that I believe, and Gödel proved, the proposition that arithmetic is, if consistent, incomplete, it would be absurd to say "*What I believe, and Gödel proved, is something I just did*."[2] The source of this absurdity is not hard to locate. Act types—like kissing Martha or predicating incompleteness of arithmetic—are either themselves a certain kind of property, or something closely akin to properties. As such, they are not the kinds of things that have truth conditions.[3]

This diagnosis of the problem suggests a natural solution. We need a replacement for act types as plausible proposition-candidates. Consider the act type of uttering 'Snow is white'. The act type of uttering this sentence can no more be identified with the sentence uttered, than the act type of predicating whiteness of snow can be identified with the proposition that snow is white. However, there are entities, closely related to these act types, with which the sentence, and the proposition, can, plausibly, be identified.

We start with a spoken utterance of 'Snow is white'. Arguably, this utterance is both an event that occurs at a particular time and place, and a token of the sentence type uttered. Thought of in this way, sentences are event types that can have multiple occurrences—like the Kentucky Derby and the Super Bowl. Just as

---

[2] See Richard Cartwright, "Propositions," in R. J. Butler, ed., *Analytical Philosophy*, 1st series (Oxford: Blackwell, 1962); reprinted in Cartwright, *Philosophical Essays* (Cambridge, MA: MIT, 1987).

[3] Examples of act types are: running, opening a door, talking to John, and predicating brilliance of someone. They are things we do. Since each one is something that can, equally well, be done by many different agents, each is an abstract object of a certain sort. Acts in this sense must be distinguished both from particular events in which agents perform them, and from the abstract type of event in which some agent performs the act. For example, the type of event in which an agent opens a door is not something we do, and so is not itself an act (act type). Below I make a case for identifying propositions with event types in which an agent predicates something of something. It is possible that Pryor had this in mind, since it is possible that by "act types," he may have meant what I call "event types."

tokens, or instances, of the horserace and the football game are particular runnings of the race, or playings of the game, so tokens of the sentence are particular utterances of it.[4] Next imagine an agent's utterance of 'Snow is white' followed by an utterance— by the same, or another, agent—of 'That's true.' In such a case, the demonstrative could be taken to refer to the utterance, to the sentence uttered, or to both. What the example illustrates is that sentences, thought of as event types, *can be bearers of truth value.*

Next consider an event in which I don't utter anything, but simply think of snow as white, thereby predicating whiteness of it. This cognition is both an event involving me that occurs at a particular time and place, and also an instance of a corresponding event type in which an agent predicates whiteness of snow. Just as the sentence 'Snow is white' can be identified with an event type of which an utterance of it is an instance, so *the proposition that snow is white* can be identified with an event type of which predicating whiteness of snow at a particular time and place is an instance. Thus, it is natural that both the event type that is the sentence 'Snow is white' and the event type that is the proposition that snow is white should be genuine bearers of truth conditions. Since this is a new way of thinking of propositions in philosophy, it may be a bit surprising to be told that they are things that occur, or have particular instances. However, I don't see this consequence as incoherent, or disqualifyingly bizarre. On the contrary, the theoretical advantages of thinking of propositions in

---

[4] The picture is complicated by the fact that some tokens of 'Snow is white' are utterances, while others are inscriptions. Perhaps, in light of this, the sentence type should be seen as a disjunction of an utterance type and an inscription type. Since I don't think the philosophical points I wish to make are compromised by this complication, I will continue to speak as if sentence types could be identified with event types the instances of which are utterances.

this way are substantial, and justify this modest extension in our view of them.

Do these propositions-*cum*-event-types exist at possible world-states at which they have no instances (because no agents perform the requisite predications)? Because they are abstract objects, it might be argued that they do. Since it is clear from their very nature that they bear the same truth conditions at all world-states at which they exist, their existence at every world-state would mean that they have the same truth conditions at every state. However, some may argue that event types exist only at world-states at which they have instances. It is important to note that even if this is so, it doesn't affect our conception of what it is for a proposition to be true at a world-state. Consider, for example, the simple proposition-*cum*-event-type, *that snow is white*, at a world-state w at which it doesn't exist because no one ever predicates anything of anything. For this proposition to be true at w is simply for it to be the case that, had w obtained, snow would have been as it is represented to be—namely white—by any possible instance of the proposition—i.e., by any possible case in which an agent predicates the property *being white* of snow. Since the satisfaction of this condition doesn't require any of the relevant predications to occur at w, the proposition that snow is white can be true at w, even if it doesn't exist at w. In short, propositions bear their truth conditions essentially, and can be evaluated with respect to every possible world-state.

In addition to bearing their truth conditions intrinsically, and unproblematically, propositions-*cum*-event-types are things with which we are readily and unmysteriously acquainted. Since the proposition that snow is white is the minimal event type in which an agent predicates whiteness of snow, and since every propositional attitude one bears to this proposition involves one's performing this predication, agents capable of being acquainted with their own cognitive processes—in the sense of being able to make them objects of their thought—will typically be capable of being similarly acquainted with the proposition that snow is white, by virtue of being acquainted with the cognitive event that is the instance of it they have brought about.[5] Given the means both of thinking of snow as white, and of becoming aware of thinking of snow in this way, agents are thereby in a position to make further predications of the content of their thought. Consequently, if, after I predicate whiteness of snow, I say to myself, "Yes, that's true," I thereby correctly predicate truth of the proposition that is the type of cognitive event I have just brought about. This result explains how agents are able to entertain compound propositions by predicating properties of their constituent propositions, which was the problem that led us to abandon the deflationary conception of propositions in search of a better alternative.

In providing the solution to this problem, the realist account of propositions inherits the virtues of the deflationary theory, without its most serious difficulties. Like the deflationary account, it provides the entities needed as contents of sentences, bearers of truth value, and objects of the attitudes required by our best semantic, pragmatic, and cognitive theories. But while the deflationary account sees nothing beyond the multiplicity of unavoidably arbitrary abstract formal structures that "play the role of propositions," the realist account views such structures as

---

[5] As with many abstract objects, acquaintance with the instances of the event types that are propositions, plus the ability to notice relevant similarities among those instances, play crucial roles in our acquaintance with the types.

merely useful theoretical devices that *represent* the real propositions to which agents bear natural cognitive relations. The labeled bracketings, or hierarchical trees, provided by linguistic and cognitive theories encode the structure and sequence of cognitive acts of predication that are necessary and sufficient for entertaining the real propositions these abstract structures represent—where entertaining such a proposition is performing the acts of predication involved in tokening the event type that it is.

This naturalized account of propositions also solves, or dissolves, the most important problems to which traditional theories of propositions give rise. Unlike the platonic epistemology required by the classic Frege-Russell account—according to which acquaintance with, and knowledge of, propositions involve an obscure sort of intellectual intuition—the epistemology of naturalized propositions sees acquaintance with, and knowledge of, propositions as rooted in acquaintance with, and knowledge of, the acts and events that make up one's cognitive life. Of course, the attribution of propositional attitudes to others, and the identification of certain propositions as the semantic contents of specific sentences, or the contents asserted by certain utterances, goes well beyond this. However, these are cases of normal empirical uncertainty, common to most ordinary judgments, and empirical theories. When propositions are properly conceived, appealing to them doesn't muddy the waters by needlessly complicating the epistemology of such judgments and theories.

Also unlike the Frege-Russell account, the cognitive-realist conception doesn't face the metaphysical pseudo-problem of "the unity of the proposition," which—though traditionally described as that of explaining how the constituents of propositions "hold together"—serves only to mask the real problem of explaining how propositions can be representational, and so have truth conditions. To the extent that the traditional account even recognizes the problem, it fails to offer a solution. Worse, it takes the mysterious, unexplained, and supposedly intrinsic representational properties of propositions to be the source from which the cognitive states of agents, and the sentences they employ, inherit their representational properties, thereby ensuring the impossibility of explaining the intentionality of anything. This, I have argued, is as avoidable as it is unacceptable. The key is to reverse our explanatory priorities. Propositions, properly conceived, are not an *independent* source of that which is representational in mind and language; rather, propositions are representational *because* of their intrinsic connection to the inherently representational cognitive events in which agents predicate some things of other things.

This conception of propositions also solves the semantic problem that prompted Donald Davidson's criticism, discussed in chapter 4, that "the one thing meanings [propositions] do not seem to do is oil the wheels of a theory of meaning." The problem is that theories assigning classical Frege-Russell propositions, or their more modern variants, to sentences don't put us in a position to understand what those sentences mean. To achieve this, information about what is predicated of what must be made explicit, from which the truth conditions of propositions can then be derived. This idea, on which the deflationary account was based, is inherited by the cognitive-realist conception of propositions—which *can* play the role of sentence meanings dreamed of by theorists since Frege, while also being epistemologically and metaphysically acceptable.

Chapter 7

Expanding the Cognitive-Realist Model

THE FOUNDATIONAL THEORY of propositions presented in the last two chapters is, I hope, attractive. However, it is very far from being established. Its most serious shortcoming is its present limited scope. In presenting the theory, I have restricted myself to propositions expressed by the simple formal language PL—a standard first-order language of the predicate calculus, augmented with modal operators and psychological attitude verbs. Although the propositions expressible in PL make up a rich and interesting class, many propositions expressible in English and other natural languages are not members of it. Since any acceptable account of what propositions are must be extendable to all propositions, it is important to indicate some of the ways by which the present semantic and foundational model can be made more expansive.

Some means of increasing its scope—e.g., adding indexicals, allowing quantifier domains to include anything we like, and adding further descriptive vocabulary to PL—are essentially trivial, and provide us with propositions the constituents of which might include just about anything. The challenging extensions involve propositions expressed by sentences containing syntactically and semantically complex expressions of various types not found in PL. The model I have so far presented has three main features: (i) every proposition is formed simply by predicating an n-place property of n arguments; (ii) every argument is either (a) a proposition formed as in (i), (b) a propositional function from objects to propositions formed as in (i), or (c) an object designated by a linguistically simple singular term; and (iii) every property is either (a) expressed by a simple nonlogical predicate, (b) expressed by a simple logical operator (modal, quantificational, or truth-functional), or (c) a complex property corresponding to a propositional function from objects to propositions formed as in (i). Though sufficient for propositions expressible in PL, models conforming to (i)–(iii) won't suffice for propositions expressed by sentences of languages with richer resources for constructing complex expressions out of simpler ones. I will illustrate this by saying a few words about complex singular terms, predicates, and quantifiers, as well as compound sentences—indicating both challenges to be overcome and some strategies for doing so. I will begin with complex singular terms, which bring with them an important conceptual extension of the basic model.

Complex Singular Terms

The difference between the contributions of simple and complex singular terms to the propositions expressed by sentences containing them is illustrated by example 1.

1a.   6 cubed > 14 squared
  b.   216 > 196

For our purposes, we will take Arabic numerals to be linguistically simple (directly referential) singular terms, in the sense of contributing their referents to the semantic contents of (or propositions expressed by) sentences containing them. By contrast, '6 cubed' and '14 squared' are linguistically complex, with '( ) squared' designating the function f_2 that assigns to any number n the result of multiplying n by n, and '(_) cubed' designating the function f_3 that assigns to any number n the result of multiplying n squared by n. Although the complex terms in (1a) are coreferential with their linguistically simple counterparts in (1b), the propositions expressed by the two sentences are different. Our semantic and foundational model must accommodate this.

Since (1b) involves only a simple 2-place predicate and a pair of linguistically simple singular terms, it fits our existing model. The proposition it expresses is, therefore, represented by the abstract structure (2), and identified with the event type in which an agent predicates the relation *being greater than* of the number 216 followed by the number 196.

2.

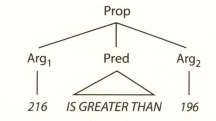

By contrast, it would seem that the proposition expressed by (1a) should be represented by the abstract structure (3).

3.

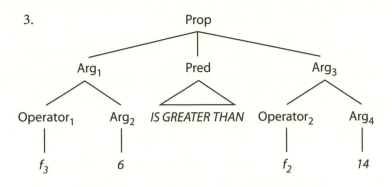

What event type should the proposition represented by (3) be identified with? Perhaps it is the event type in which one predicates *being greater than* of the pair consisting of whatever number is the result of applying f_3 to 6 followed by whatever number is the result of applying f_2 to 14. However, since $f_3(6) = 216$ and $f_2(14) = 196$, this characterization of the proposition expressed by (1a) is problematic. Rather, it is problematic, if, as may seem natural, one assumes that $\ulcorner$X predicates P of $\alpha \ldots \beta\urcorner$ is an extensional context (for the positions occupied by $\alpha \ldots \beta$). On this assumption, anyone who predicates *being greater than* of 216 followed by 196 also predicates it of the result of applying f_3 to 6 followed by the result of applying f_2 to 14, and vice versa. Since this yields the incorrect result that anyone who entertains one of the two propositions also entertains the other, either the proposition expressed by (1a) has been identified with the wrong event type, or predication contexts aren't extensional (or both).

Perhaps the proposition expressed by (1a) should be identified with the complex event type of (i) applying the cubing function f_3 to the number 6, (ii) applying the squaring function f_2 to the number 14, and then (iii) predicating the relation *being greater than* of the pair consisting of the result of (i) followed by the result of (ii). This has the satisfying result that the propositions expressed by (1a) and (1b) are clearly different, and that entertaining the latter is not sufficient for entertaining the former. However, if predication constructions are extensional, we still get the unwanted result that entertaining the former proposition is sufficient for entertaining the latter.

Nor will it do to identify the proposition expressed by (1a) with that expressed by (1c)—namely the event type in which an agent predicates the relation *being a pair of numbers the cube of the first of which is greater than the square of the second.*

1c. λxy [x cubed > y squared] 6, 14

Although not an unreasonable idea about the content of the proposition, this proposal gives no account of how the complex relation said to be predicated is determined from the structure and constituents of (1a). According to it, the proposition expressed by (1a) and (1c) is represented by the abstract structure (4a), in which g assigns to any numbers n and m the abstract structure (4b).

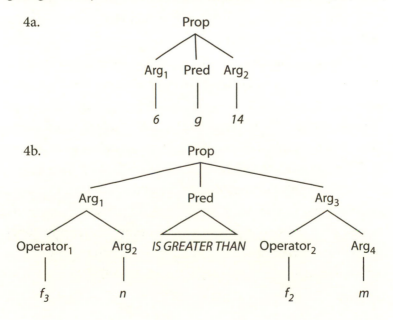

The problem is that (4b) is precisely the kind of structure we are searching for a way to understand. Without such an understanding, we don't know how to interpret (4a).

Given these results, we have little recourse but to revisit the second of my three alternatives. The proposition expressed by (1a), and corresponding to the abstract structure (3), is the complex event type of (i) thinking of the cubing function f_3 and the number 6, and *applying* the former to the latter, (ii) thinking of the squaring function f_2 and the number 14, and again *applying* the former to the latter, and (iii) predicating the relation *being greater than* of the result of applying f_3 to 6, followed by the result of applying f_2 to 14. By contrast, the proposition expressed by (1b) is the event type of thinking of the numbers 216 and 196, and predicating *being greater than* of the former, followed by the latter. Since these event types are different, the propositions are different. Since entertaining the latter doesn't require thinking about f_2, f_3, 6, or 14, or of *applying* any function to an argument, it is obvious that entertaining proposition (1b) doesn't involve entertaining proposition (1a).

If it were the case that having a function f and potential argument a in mind, and *applying* f to a counted as *thinking about v*, or *having v in mind*, where v = f(a), then we might still get the unwanted result that entertaining (1a) involved entertaining (1b). But it doesn't. To *apply* f to a is not to calculate the value of f at a, but merely to take a as an *argument* of f. This cognitive act—of *applying* a function to something—is akin to the act of *predicating* a property of something. To *predicate* a property *being P* of an object o is to represent o as *being P*; to *apply* a function f to o is to represent o as something on which f operates. Just as the representation of o as *being P* may determine a truth value, without one who predicates that property of o knowing what the resulting truth value is, so the representation of o as input to the f-operation may determine a value, without one who *applies* f to o knowing what the resulting value is. Thus, one who entertains proposition (1a) need not have 216 and 196 (which are the values of the function f_3 at the argument 6, and the function f_2 at the argument 14, respectively) in mind. As a result, entertaining proposition (1a) does *not* involve entertaining proposition (1b).

This result is more far-reaching than it might at first seem to be. In introducing the notion of *applying a function to an argument*, we have expanded our conception of the cognitive acts constituting propositions in an important way. Propositions are no longer restricted to event types in which an agent (merely) performs a structured sequence of predications. In addition, they now include event types in which an agent performs a structured sequence of acts that include functional applications along with predications. Expanding the model in this way brings with it the need to consider cases in which agents apply functions to arguments for which the functions are undefined.

Consider a simplified example in which two people, A and B, are talking about the arithmetic of the rational numbers. Although the domain of discourse is restricted to the rationals, at one point A, who is ignorant of the fact that the square-root function is undefined for the argument 2, expresses his sincere belief by assertively uttering (1d).

1d. The square root of 2 is greater than 1.

Although false, the sentence uttered is meaningful, and so expresses a proposition—which A asserts and believes. To entertain this proposition, one must apply the square-root function to the number 2, which both A and B do. However, this isn't the whole story. In addition, one must predicate being greater than of *the result of this application*, followed by the number 1. However, since there is no (rational) square root of 2, there would seem to be no such thing as *the result of applying the square-root function to 2*. How, then, is the proposition expressed by (1d) to be understood?

To answer this question we need to clarify an issue in the logic of predication ascriptions that we have not previously had to face. Is α exportable from the position it occupies in (5a) to its position in (5b); in other words, does (5a) entail (5b)?

5a.   Agent A predicates property P of . . . α . . .

  b.   For some x (x = α & agent A predicates property P of . . . x . . .)

If we assume that (5a) does entail (5b), then we cannot maintain that entertaining the proposition expressed by (1d) requires one to predicate *being greater than* of the result of applying the (rational) square-root function to 2, followed by the number 1, while recognizing, as we must, that there is no (rational) number that is the result of applying the function to that argument. Since we don't want one analysis of propositions involving the application of functions that are undefined at the relevant arguments, and a different analysis of propositions in which the functions are defined, this negative conclusion generalizes to examples like (1a).

Faced with this result, it may seem tempting to replace acts of *predication* in the analysis with acts of *intending to predicate*. On this imagined revision, the proposition expressed by (1d) is the event type in which an agent (i) *applies* the (rational) square-root function to the number 2, and (ii) *intends to predicate* the property being greater than of *the result of that application*, followed by the number 1. However, this won't do. Although (ii) may sound like an accurate description of what A does when A entertains, asserts, and believes the proposition, it is not an accurate description of what B does—knowing that there is no (rational) square root of 2, and no relevant pair for *being greater than* to be predicated of—when B entertains, disbelieves, and predicates *being believed by A*, of the very same proposition. Thus, substituting 'intending to predicate' for 'predicate' in the analysis of propositions involving functional application does *not* solve the problem created by taking predication ascriptions of the form (5a) to entail corresponding ascriptions of the form (5b).

The correct solution is to recognize that no such entailment relation holds. In this respect, the verb 'predicate', as used in our theory of propositions, is analogous to *intensional transitive verbs* like 'worship' and 'look for'. As we all know, Juan may look for the fountain waters from which will bring one eternal youth, even if there is no such thing, and John may worship the being described in the Bible who created heaven and earth, and rewards those who believe in him with eternal life, even if no such being exists. Similarly, one can predicate a property P of the result of applying f to o, even if there is no object which is the value of f at o. Like an intensional transitive, which expresses a relation between an agent and a content that reflects something about the agent's attitude toward, or cognitive perspective on, the content, the verb 'predicate' expresses a cognitive relation between an agent, a property, and a content. Thus, although it may initially seem surprising that statements of the form (5a) can be true, even in cases in which the corresponding statements (5b) are false, in the end this is explicable. On one point, however, there must be no confusion. Whereas the existence of a proposition that consists simply of applying f to o and predicating P of the result does *not* require f to be defined for o, the truth of the proposition does.

This analysis, adopted for the propositions expressed by (1a) and (1d), extends to sentences containing Frege-style singular definite descriptions $\ulcorner \iota x\ Gx \urcorner$. These descriptions are complex singular terms in which the operator 'ιx' denotes a function f_ι that maps the propositional function f_g expressed by the formula Gx onto an object o iff o is the unique object to which f_g assigns a true proposition; otherwise f_ι is undefined. Thus, the proposition expressed by (6) is represented by the abstract structure (7), and identified with the complex event type of (i) thinking of the iota function f_ι and the function f_g (expressed by Gx), while taking the latter to be the argument of the former, and (ii) predicating the property *Fness* (expressed by F) of the value of f_ι at the argument f_g.

6.   F (ιx Gx)

7.

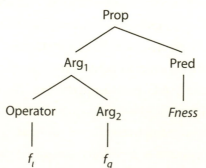

This proposition is distinct from the proposition expressed by $\ulcorner Fn \urcorner$, where n is a (directly referential) name the referent of which $= f_\iota(f_g)$. Moreover, entertaining either of these propositions is independent of entertaining the other. Finally, although the truth of the proposition requires f_ι to be defined at the argument

f_g, its existence doesn't. These are just the results we need, if the semantic and foundational model presented here is to remain viable.

Complex Predicates and Compound Sentences

The language PL used to illustrate our foundational theory of propositions shares with the predicate calculus the familiar treatment of negation, conjunction, and disjunction as exclusively sentential operators. This contrasts with natural language in which other, subsentential constituents are available to be negated, conjoined, or disjoined. The inclusiveness of natural language on this point can be accommodated by our theory of propositions. One advantage of showing this is to highlight, and hopefully transcend, a potentially worrisome limitation of the account of truth-functionally compound propositions given so far.

Imagine a speaker who understands a number of predicates, and is able to use them to predicate the properties they express of entities of various kinds. For example, the speaker knows that 'is red' is a predicate used to predicate the property *being red* of things, while 'is round' is used to predicate the property *being round*. Learning to negate, conjoin, and disjoin predicates, the speaker will come to know that 'is not red' and 'is not round' are predicates used to predicate the compound properties *not being red* and *not being round*, that 'is red and round' is a predicate phrase used to predicate the compound property *being red and round*, and that 'is red or round' predicates the compound property *being red or round*. These compound properties are complex, the constituents of which are the simple properties redness and roundness, plus the negation, conjunction, and disjunction operators. Thus, to entertain the proposition *that o isn't red and round* is to predicate *not being red and round* of o—where predicating that compound property requires (a) having the properties *being red* and *being round* in mind, (b) conjoining them—which can be thought of as applying the property-conjoining operator $CONJ_{Pred-Op}$—to get the property *being red and round*, and (c) negating this property—which involves applying the property-negating operator $NEG_{Pred-Op}$—to get the negative compound property that is predicated of o. The proposition resulting from this predication is, of course, true iff o has the property *not being red and round* iff o doesn't have the property *being red and round* iff either o doesn't have the property *being red* or o doesn't have the property *being round* iff either o isn't red or o isn't round.

Next consider the use of negation, conjunction, and disjunction as sentential operators, which is how they occur in PL. According to the semantic analysis given in earlier chapters, truth-functionally compound sentences containing these operators express compound propositions that predicate truth, or untruth, of their constituent propositions. This may seem surprising on two counts. First, simple atomic propositions, like the proposition *that o is red,* don't predicate truth of anything, nor does entertaining them require an agent to do so. Why then should the propositions *that o is red and o* is round* and *that o is red or o* is round* be thought to predicate truth of anything? Second, it is a consequence of treating truth-functional compounds as they are in PL that agents who don't possess the concept of truth can't entertain, or bear propositional attitudes to, truth-functionally compound propositions. This may be all right for PL, which is merely a stipulated language. However, since acquiring the concept of truth requires a considerable amount of prior language learning, one might wonder whether entertaining negative, conjunctive, and disjunctive propositions really requires first having the concept of truth.

If it is required, then the acquisition of the concept of truth must proceed in stages. The first stage presupposes familiarity with a set of basic, non-compound propositions, leading to the abstraction of a property T that one is justified in believing a proposition p to have when and only when one was justified in believing p. At the second stage, which can be repeated *ad infinitum*, the agent entertains compound propositions that involve predicating T, or the negation of this property, of propositions available at previous stages. Our full-fledged concept of truth is that which emerges from indefinitely many applications of this process. If something along these lines is feasible, then the treatment of truth-functional propositions in PL isn't ruled out by worries about truth.

However, it is not obviously required either. Consider the case of conjunction and disjunction as predicate operators. If English speakers can form compound predicates by using these operators to conjoin and disjoin simpler ones they already understand, it is not clear why they shouldn't be able to do something similar to form truth-functionally compound sentences. On this account, when 'and' and 'or' are used as predicate operators, they express $CONJ_{Pred-Op}$ and $DISJ_{Pred-Op}$, which operate on pairs of properties to form compound conjunctive and disjunctive properties; when they are used as sentential connectives, they express $CONJ_{Prop-Op}$ and $DISJ_{Prop-Op}$, which operate on pairs of antecedently entertained propositions to form compound conjunctive and disjunctive propositions. If, as previously indicated, truth is not predicated or presupposed in the former case, there seems to be no compelling reason why it has to be in the latter case.

On this picture, a conjunctive or disjunctive proposition is not an event type in which an agent *predicates* anything of the individual conjuncts or disjuncts. Rather, it is an event type in which an agent performs the act of *conjoining* or *disjoining* them (in addition to whatever acts of predication are needed to entertain the conjuncts or disjuncts). In principle, negation could be treated similarly. Whether or not we should think of the propositions expressed by negations of English sentences in this way is an open question. Although negative particles appear in a variety of syntactic environments in English, the only expressions that can be used to negate arbitrary declarative sentences are 'it is not true that' and its synonym 'it is not the case that'—both of which presuppose the notion of truth. For example, one who wants to negate the English sentences ⌜P and Q⌝ or ⌜P or Q⌝ has little choice but to prefix the sentence to be negated with one of these two negative phrases, thereby, apparently, predicating untruth of the proposition the original sentence expresses. Thus, the general means of expressing negative propositions by negating sentences in English seem to be quite similar to the one in PL.

QUANTIFICATION

The account of quantification I have given is a variant of the standard and now widely accepted Frege-Russell view, according to which (8a) expresses a proposition that predicates the property of being *sometimes true* of the propositional function g that assigns to any object o the proposition that predicates F-hood of o; (8b) expresses the proposition that predicates *being always true* of g.[1]

---

[1] In this section I use 'F' and 'A', both in the text and in examples, as schematic letters.

8a. $\exists x\ Fx$ / Something is F

  b. $\forall x\ Fx$ / Everything is F

Simplifying a bit, and taking the role of propositional functions as representing properties at face value, we may say that (8a) expresses the proposition that *being F* is instantiated, while (8b) expresses the proposition that *being F* is universally instantiated. What exactly are these properties, *being instantiated* and *being universally instantiated*? The natural answer is that they are the properties *being true of something* and *being true of everything*. On this understanding, the Frege-Russell analysis tells us that (8a) expresses the proposition that *being F* is true of something, while (8b) expresses the proposition that *being F* is true of everything.

Although this analysis gets the truth conditions of quantified sentences right, its account of propositional structure is problematic. It identifies the proposition *that everything is F*, expressed by (8b), with

8b₁. the proposition: the property *being F* is true of everything

which is also expressed by sentence (8b₂),

8b₂. The property *being F* is true of everything (equivalently: everything is such that the property *being F* is true of it).

However, since this sentence itself involves universal quantification, the Frege-Russell analysis ought to apply again, this time identifying the proposition (8b₁), supposedly expressed by sentence (8b), with the proposition (8b₃),

8b$_3$. the proposition: the property *being such that being F is true of it* is true of everything (or equivalently, the proposition: the property *instantiating the property being F* is true of everything)

and so on *ad infinitum*. The problem, of course, is that each iteration of the analysis seems to yield a different proposition, attributing *being true of everything* to a new, and even higher-order, property. Since it is an essential feature of structured propositions that they are individuated by what they predicate of what, there seems to be no plausible way to deny that each proposition in the hierarchy differs from all those that follow it—even though it is both necessarily and apriori equivalent to them. If this is right, it is a *reductio ad absurdum* of the Frege-Russell analysis employed here, since the proposition expressed by (8b) can't be identical with two different propositions, let alone an infinite hierarchy of them.

The same result can be achieved using propositional functions plus the property *being always true*, instead of properties plus the higher-order property *being true of everything*—provided that the property *being always true* is identified with *being a propositional function that assigns a true proposition to every object*. Interestingly, Russell himself did not fall into this trap. Instead, he took *being always true* to be primitive.[2] However, it is hard to credit this. For one thing, it seems to get the order of analysis wrong. It isn't universal quantification that we don't understand without an explanation. What we don't understand without an explanation is what it means to say that a propositional function *is always true*, or that a property *is universally instantiated*. However, if

---

[2] Russell, "On Denoting," *Mind* 14, no. 56 (1905), 479–93, at p. 480. Russell defines *being sometimes true* in terms of *being always true*, which he takes to be primitive.

these properties aren't primitive, but rather are analyzed in terms of universal quantification, then we can't analyze universal quantification in terms of them.

Realizing this, one might be tempted to revert to the view that the property *being always true* (or *being universally instantiated*) must be primitive after all, despite the unintuitiveness of this position. However, the problem with it is worse than it seems. It is crucial to the conception of propositions outlined here that their truth conditions be straightforwardly derivable from a specification of what properties they predicate of what arguments. For this we need to be able to take principles like (i) and (ii) for granted.

(i)   A proposition that predicates *being always true* of a propositional function g is true iff g assigns a true proposition to *every object.*

(ii)   A proposition that predicates *being universally instantiated* of a property P is true iff P is true of *every object.*

Without a justification of these principles, our assignments of truth conditions to the Frege-Russell propositions putatively expressed by universally quantified sentences will not, as they must, follow from the nature of the propositions themselves, but will, at best, depend on an independent and unexplained understanding of the sentences that express them. Since this is intolerable, one should, it seems, take *assigning a truth to every object* to be *what it means* for a propositional function to be *always true*—and, correspondingly, take *being true of every object* to be *what it means* for a property to be *universally instantiated.* If one does this, then the justification of (i) and (ii) will take care of itself. From those who would foreswear this justification, in the name of preserving the

Frege-Russell analysis, we must ask for an alternate justification. It is hard to see what it might be.

There is, of course, always the expedient of defining universal quantification in terms of existential quantification—i.e., of identifying the proposition *the property being F is universally instantiated* with the proposition *the property not being F isn't instantiated*, while taking *being instantiated* to be a genuine primitive. However, in addition to being dubious, this strategy leaves the needed principle (iii) unexplained.

(iii)   A proposition that predicates *being instantiated* of a property P is true iff P is true of *some (at least one) object*.

Worse, the strategy of positing primitive higher-level properties corresponding to either or both the unrestricted existential quantifier and the unrestricted universal quantifier doesn't generalize very well to the full range of quantificational cases that need to be covered.

In order to be adequate, any analysis of unrestricted quantification in the examples in (8) must carry over to the examples of restricted quantification in (9).

9a.   Most A's are F.
 b.   Many A's are F.
 c.   Few A's are F.
 d.   At least / at most / exactly n A's are F.

The most natural extension of the Frege-Russell analysis assigns these sentences propositions in which the higher-order properties—*being true of most, many, few, at least / at most / exactly n of the things that are A*—are predicated of the property *being F*, or, equivalently, propositions in which the higher-order properties— *assigning a true proposition to most, many, few, at least / at most / exactly n of the things that are A's*—are predicated of the propositional function expressed by *Fx*. However, if the very quantifiers used to define these higher-order properties are the ones for which the properties are supposed to supply an analysis, then the *reductio ad absurdum* of the classical Frege-Russell analysis of (8b), provided by $(8b_1–b_3)$, will be recapitulated for the extension of the analysis to the sentences in (9). Moreover, in this case the alternative of defining the needed higher-order properties in terms of instantiation, existential quantification, or universal quantification isn't available. Although the higher-order properties could, perhaps, be taken as primitive, this option is even less attractive than the idea that the higher-order properties introduced by the unrestricted existential and universal quantifiers are. For one thing, there are too many higher-order properties introduced by complex quantifier phrases for it to be plausible that they are all primitive. For another, we have no independent, antecedently understood, expressions on hand to specify these properties.

Consider (9a), for example. One strategy that is sometimes employed is to treat this sentence as expressing the proposition that predicates a higher-order relation—*Most?*—of the pair consisting of the property A followed by the property F. What can the proponent of the Frege-Russell analysis say to identify this relation, other than that it is the semantic content of 'most'? One has to say something to justify (iv), which is required to derive the truth conditions of the proposed proposition from this account of its structure.

(iv)   The relation *Most₂* is true of the pair <property 1, property 2> iff most things of which property 1 is true are things of which property 2 is true.

The natural justification of (iv) is provided by the definition of *Most₂* given by (v).

(v)   *Most₂* is the relation of being a pair of properties <property 1, property 2> such that most things that instantiate property 1 instantiate property 2.

However, (v) is precisely what one cannot say if all sentences containing 'most'-quantifiers are to be analyzed as expressing propositions involving the higher-order relation. Although the proponent of the Frege-Russell analysis may wish to reject (v), to take *Most₂* to be primitive, and to search for some other, so far unspecified, justification for (iv), we have been given no reason to believe that such a strategy can succeed.

The conclusion of this argument is disturbing: neither the examples in (9), nor the English equivalents of those in (8), express propositions that predicate higher-order properties of lower-order properties, or propositional functions. If this is right, we need a new account of quantification not based on the Frege-Russell model. This doesn't mean that the semantic theory of PL given in previous chapters is inaccurate, or that PL isn't a possible language. The Frege-Russell readings of (8a,b) are coherent, and are certainly learnable by possible speakers. What is in doubt is that what passes for quantification in PL really is quantification, as we all antecedently understand it in natural language. If, as I now suspect, it isn't, then there is a serious gap in the foundational account of propositions I have offered.

Perhaps that gap can be filled by expanding the range of cognitive acts involved in entertaining various propositions to include quantificational acts of some sort, in addition to the acts of (i) predicating properties, (ii) applying functions to arguments, (iii) negating, conjoining, and disjoining properties to form compound properties, and (iv) negating, conjoining, or disjoining propositions to form compound propositions. However, if this is the direction in which to look for a solution, I don't see precisely how it should go. Thus, the apparent failure of the Frege-Russell treatment of quantification remains a serious unsolved problem for the foundational theory of propositions offered here—as it does for other, competing, theories of structured propositions.

Index